TABLE OF CONTENTS

Acknowledgements................................. v
Introduction..ix

CHAPTER 1 The Multigenerational Covenant Family..... 25
  Hermeneutics for a Theology of the Covenant Family
  Family Model Alternatives
  The Biblical Foundations
    The Covenant
    Key Scripture Passages
  Defining a Christian Multigenerational Family
    Cultural Transmission
    Covenant Foundation
    Dominion is the Mission
    Four Components of Christian Multigenerational Families

CHAPTER 2 The Multigenerational Family Blueprint..... 57
  Sample Outlines of a Family Constitution
  Family Documents Portfolio

CHAPTER 3 The Family Mission..................... 69
  Covenant
  Beliefs and Values
  The Family Vision Statement
  Considerations Before Drafting the Family Mission Statement
    Common vs. Unique Elements of a Christian Family Mission

Is The Family Mission Discovered or Determined?
  Process versus Purpose
  Drafting Your Family Mission Statement
  Sample Family Mission Statements
  Objectives, Strategy, Tactics, and Family Aspirations

CHAPTER 4 The Family "Assets and Balance Sheet" 99

CHAPTER 5 Family Governance and Succession 107
  Succession and Membership
  Sphere Sovereignty and Jurisdiction
  Transition to Adulthood
  Governance System Options
  Our Family's Governance Assumptions
    The Firstborn
    On Daughters and Inheritance
    First Generation Estate and Family Council
    Clan Governance
    A Confederated Republic or a Covenantal Aristocracy?
  Alliances and Treaties
  Theory on Multiple Covenant Relationships
  Conflict Resolution

CHAPTER 6 A Look Ahead. 136
  Family Discipleship Aimed at Generational Succession
  Building and Preserving Generational Wealth
  The Horizontal Family: Extended Family, Clan, and Tribe
  Roles
  Generational Growth and Maturity
  The Generational Family in Kingdom Context

Appendix. 145
  Family Discipleship for Multigenerational Families

Bibliography. 157
End Notes 162

Families in Covenant Succession

A Manual for Muligenerational Faithfulness

by Jason Diffner

Copyright © 2014 by Jason Diffner

Families in Covenant Succession
A Manual for Multigenerational Faithfulness
by Jason Diffner

Printed in the United States of America

ISBN 9781498411370

All rights reserved solely by the author. The author guarantees all contents are original and do not infringe upon the legal rights of any other person or work. No part of this book may be reproduced in any form without the permission of the author. The views expressed in this book are not necessarily those of the publisher.

Scripture quotations taken from the English Standard Version (ESV). Copyright © 2001 by Crossway, a publishing ministry of Good News Publishers. Used by permission. All rights reserved.

www.xulonpress.com

ACKNOWLEDGEMENTS
✣

This is my first book and I have greatly anticipated the opportunity to thank the many individuals who, in some form or fashion, have helped with this work. To the reader, I want to emphasize that this acknowledgement portion of the book is very important to me and therefore is more important to you than you might realize. Readers better understand an author's message when they know what he is most thankful for.

I first want to thank God my Father, and His Son, my Redeemer, the Lord Jesus Christ, and the Holy Spirit, sent by the Father and Son, enabling me, in grace, to do any service acceptable in His sight. My King, the Lord Jesus, is precious to me and I stand dumbfounded before the greatness of His ineffable majesty. While I was spitting in the face of God, He died for me! He has given me the grace of faith to believe the unbelievable – that I am an adopted son of the Father, a servant in His Kingdom. Any goodness this book yields in His Kingdom is His work – I am but His vessel.

My wife, Stacie, is an indispensable help in this work. The majority of this book was written during a time of unemployment. My guess is that many a wife would find it difficult to encourage a husband to risk energies on writing during unemployment. Stacie, however, had more faith than me and encouraged me in the work during a long and trying period. I am thankful for Stacie being the first editor of the book; many sentences and paragraphs are more hers than mine.

I cannot express in words the gratitude I feel toward my parents, Dan and Dawn Diffner. They raised me in godly, covenantal nurture. They are the primary tools God has used in whatever maturity I possess. My wife recently was sharing with me how she is mourning the transition of how our older children become less physically affectionate with her. We both miss the big, long hugs we still enjoy with our little ones. I want my parents to know that the shameless child in me still wants to give them a big, long hug of thankfulness.

I want to thank Jeremy Pryor. You will learn more about Jeremy in the opening of the book. Without his ministry of teaching about multigenerational families, this book would have never been written. His faithful obedience to the Lord in teaching on this vital subject is what started my journey into understanding and practicing multigenerational family faithfulness.

I want to thank Gary Duff, elder at Dominion Covenant Church in Omaha, Nebraska. Gary found my contact information on a website while I was just starting to write the book (during my season of unemployment), and called me one day. Gary let me know that he, and the community of churches he fellowships with, are eager to learn more about multigenerational families. He has been my primary champion and encourager throughout the writing of the book. I am highly suspicious that without his encouragement, the book may have never been written. Thank you, Gary.

Thanks are due to my brother, James Diffner, my brother-in-law, Josh Frost, and my friend, Adam Rust for their input and interaction with the development of this work.

I want to thank Geoff Botkin (www.westernconservatory.com). Geoff and his family have been our primary model for what a dominion-minded, multigenerational family looks

Acknowledgements

like. Through his teaching ministry, he has been a critical source of instruction and inspiration for me and my family.

Finally, I want to thank the following friends for donating $200 or more to my RocketHub campaign to help provide funding for the publishing of this book: the Buckingham family, Sean and Katelyn Cohen, Jeff Williams, Jennie Putnam, Jeremy Pryor, Joseph Graham, and Chris Zimmerman. I want to thank all my other RocketHub funders as well – you know who you are. Thank you.

INTRODUCTION

The Back Story

In 2008 I experienced a major conversion in my understanding of family. My beautiful wife, Stacie, and I had three young boys at the time. I had always been a man who held strong convictions about spending my primary energies on significant and meaningful work for the advancement of the Kingdom of God. There was theology and culture to study. Books to be written. Classes to be taught. And here I was with a nine-to-five office job and a family with three growing boys. Because my theological presuppositions about family were built on Western individualism, I experienced my family (whom I dearly loved) as the main barrier to, and competitor with, my ambitions to do Kingdom work. Where was the time to study, to write, to teach? I am ashamed to say it now, but while I loved and enjoyed my family dearly, my duty to be responsibly present to my children was the biggest source of bitterness in my life. I could not understand why God put a passion for Kingdom work in my heart and then "burdened" me with a family such that I had not the time nor energy to do the work I felt needed to be done.

There was another backdrop relevant to the change that was about to occur in my thinking. For as long as I can remember in my adult life, I had always dreamt of building a little "family economic empire" for the purpose of passing on to my children. This may look like multigenerational thinking, and it was to some degree, but it was not rooted in a biblical theology. I imagine many (most?) fathers hold some form of this thought in their hearts. Like them, for me it was more instinctual than anything else. Untethered from biblical foundations, this instinct can only be perverted into a selfish drive for "Babylon-building." There is, however, a godly, creational source for this instinct in men. It is the dominion mandate to be fruitful and exercise godly rule of the earth.

It was in this context that I attended a training hosted by my friend, Jeremy Pryor, titled, *Building Family Teams*. He told us that the reason there is not an elaborate teaching on family life in the New Testament is that Jesus and the apostles knew that the Old Testament (Hebrew Scriptures) had the foundational principles for shaping family life that Christians were presumed to rely on. A Jewish family, then and now, conceived of their family life multi-generationally, from ancient past to the distant future. A Jewish mindset thinks, "I am a descendent of Abraham. Our family is preparing for the Messiah ..." In contrast, the Western-American mindset thinks something like this: "I was born in 1975. My family is preparing to go to Yellowstone this summer ..." The Hebrew mindset of what is included in family life extends to *every* area of human activity: education, politics, culture, finances, work, technology, etc. All of life is integrated in, through, and with the family. While there is always individual expression, it is first and foremost manifested through the family.

Jeremy went on to explain how American (Western) fathers typically experience a disconnect with Western family culture. While not necessarily a central experience of every Western father, for most there exists a mindset where children are felt to be liabilities in terms of both time and money. He just addressed the biggest source of bitterness in my life. He had my ears!

Introduction

The message continued like this. Men (and fathers especially) are designed to be adventurous, "mini-empire" builders (the instinct rooted in the Genesis 1 dominion mandate). There is little in the Western family model that corresponds with this instinct in fathers. The Hebrew family model does, however, correspond to this instinct. God gave families a dominion task. The Hebrew-minded family is on a generational-enduring mission to serve the kingdom of God. That mission touches everything and therefore informs how they educate, work, spend their leisure time, etc. They know where certain mission goals realistically will not be realized in their own lifetimes, let alone their children's. But they can work in such a way to see those goals realized in future generations. This idea of seeing family as a stewardship to invest in God's kingdom multi-generationally was absolutely inspiring to me. It gave my instincts for multi-generational economic improvement of the family the Kingdom context it needed. Ultimately, I realized that my humble ambitions could be made *exponentially more effective* for the Kingdom of God precisely *through* my multigenerational family, rather than just through my own little lifetime. I was sold!

To share the immediate impact this training had on me, I had been in great tension about whether to continue with the adoption of a daughter from China that was extending into a multi-year wait. Because of the bitterness that I mentioned above, I was "done with having kids." After that training, my angst about having more children was gone. And it wasn't just that the angst was gone. I was eager to start having more children. Talk about a radical change in perspective on a big subject in such a short amount of time! To my wife's delight, the adoption continued and we were blessed with the birth of our son, Justus, prior to Elia joining our family.

Ever since that day, I have been an avid student of the subject of multigenerational families. I read every book I could find on the subject. Within a year I had a "book's worth" of ideas and content in my head. What I found was that all the books that spoke of the very *practical* tools for building multigenerational families were written only by secular authors. While many of those practical tools are applicable to Christian families, these authors inevitably convey ideas that are incompatible with Christian faith. It became clear to me that instruction on the practical tools for building multigenerational families written from a Christian perspective was needed. Hence, this book.

This book is unique in the multigenerational family literature for a second reason beyond being an explicitly Christian book on the subject. All the secular books on the multigenerational family assume a family is starting with a founding family who created a significant fortune. There's "seed money" for all sorts of goodies! In this book, I'm assuming the largest constituency is middle-aged, middle-class families. In other words, the "family wealth" has to be built first before the more mature legal and financial instruments need to be employed.

There's actually an advantage to this situation (starting a multigenerational family before substantive wealth has been built). From my research, it appears that for more than half of the families of wealth founders, the wealth ends up turning siblings against each other. They did not grow up in the context of a multigenerational *spiritual* vision and mission that was oriented outside of themselves. In contrast, for siblings who spend their lifetimes building "clan wealth" as an expression of their spiritual mission, the money issues are largely taken care of before the wealth is even there.

Thesis

What is my intention with this book? What do I hope it will do for readers? If the book could be summarized in thesis form, it would sound something like this: Christians today are, by and large, operating their families on a culturally Western,

Introduction

and therefore individualistic, platform (in this model, the purpose of the family is to provide a basis for individual achievement and expression). Due to cultural influences of the past 200 years, they have "forgotten" that there is a biblical mode of family life that is contrary to this individualistic assumption. The biblical platform of family is, first and foremost, covenantal, and because it is covenantal, it is multigenerational.

Individual families (nuclear families, as we call them today) are stewards of a multigenerational family that exists throughout multiple generations, identified by a common covenant faithfully transmitted from generation to generation. They are to see themselves as trustees of an unimaginably valuable family culture that has been built and preserved for hundreds of years. These families hold a reverent fear of mishandling that trust and the consequences it would mean for their descendants.

My first aim in this book is to convince you of this multigenerational model of family. The vast majority of Christians need to convert how they are operating their families on the macro scale. Once this paradigm shift has been adopted, it has a host of implications. Those implications become multigenerational disciplines that families create and practice. The second aim of the book is to train families in those disciplines and practices. Those disciplines include:
1. The creation of a family mission statement, governance policies and constitution;
2. A comprehensive family discipleship plan that includes training in subjects relevant to generational-transference; and
3. A comprehensive family wealth-building and preservation plan.

Or, to put it in an abbreviated summary, multigenerational family disciplines that include the creation and practice of a Governance Plan, a Discipleship Plan, and an Economic Plan.

The concept of a multigenerational family can be a tricky one, as you're dealing with an abstract future. Most of the work of a multigenerational family takes place in a living, breathing, nuclear family through common Christian discipleship. Necessarily, therefore, the subject of building Christian multigenerational families must address family discipleship. However, have you noticed that there are not very many self-conscious, mature, multi-generational (beyond the third generation) Christian families? In other words, do you know of a Christian family today that can say something like this: "....Yeah, our family has been living out this mission [fill in the blank] ever since great, great, great, great grandpa Smith started things off 300 years ago. Well, not just my family, but the 200 other families in our clan as well"? If you think this sounds "crazy," you need to read the story of Jonadab in the Bible (Jeremiah 35). The point is, "common family discipleship" does not, by itself, produce long-lived multigenerational families. Ironically, most of the people writing on this subject today are not believers, but the tools they know need to be applied also need to be applied to Christian families — constitutions, trusts, governance policies, etc. We Christians, however, have an advantage — we have the covenant! We have the very blessing of God upon families who faithfully abide by His covenant.

Getting back to my point. This book, while grounding the Christian family in the necessary theology of covenant families, is primarily a manual on the practices that enable families to transmit their family identity and mission across multiple generations – across hundreds of years.

At many points, the subject of multigenerational families inevitably draws us to consider future generations far removed from us. Our present cultural mindset has a hard time thinking about the abstraction of future generations. While reading a particular subject in the book, if you find yourself thinking, *"What does this have to do with me and my family on a practical level?"* there is a good chance you are just experiencing the present-orientation buried in the social-psyche of our age. If you find yourself with those thoughts, I recommend imagining what your family will look like in a fourth generation, mature form. At that point, the previously seeming irrelevant subject should begin making more sense. Example – the subject of managing multiple trusts among multiple nuclear families is not going to be something that your nuclear family is going to have to practically deal with in your own generation. However, Lord willing, your fourth-generation descendants will. While you won't be actively *managing* such complexities in your lifetime, you should begin *planning* for them for the sake of your descendants.

After researching this subject for so many years, I can lapse into assuming believers have at least a rudimentary understanding of what a multigenerational family is. However, experience has taught me that this is not the case. In the first chapter, we'll begin to delve into the details of what a Christian multigenerational family entails. To help jumpstart your thinking (and hopefully inspiration), I wanted to share a few relevant quotes to introduce what Christian multigenerational families are all about:

> The truth of generational transfer is built upon the principle of being a bridge generation, not a terminal generation. Nearly every generation for the last one hundred years has said they are the terminal generation. That is, they thought they were the generation that would witness the *Second Coming* of the Lord. Consequently, they did very little to take dominion and had very little to pass on to the generations to come. The problem is the years have come and gone and we are still here on earth. In the meantime we have not occupied until Jesus comes, and as a result we have lost the territories of universities and business, the ruling of the nations, the arts, etc.

The church is not to live as the terminal generation; it is to live as a bridge generation, a generation between what was and what is to come. A bridge generation maintains a keen sense of responsibility both to the generations before and to the generations to come. It possesses both an historic accountability and a futuristic accountability.[1]

If you were to assess the fruit of Abraham's life, what percentage of his fruitfulness was achieved by all the work he did during his life versus what he accomplished through the single act of having Isaac? The comparison is almost absurd. Virtually all his fruitfulness came through Isaac.[2]

How many activities in your typical week are focused on multiplication? Family activities like having children, adopting children, training children and grandchildren, developing repeatable family traditions are all highly fruitful and if done well, *will outlive you by many centuries*. And this, by the way, is the secret to fathers falling in love with their families. Once fathers truly grasp the insignificance of identifying with their work and the lasting significance of raising a family *their hearts will finally come home* (italics mine).[3]

This Book a Foundation for an Anticipated Expansion

This book will be a foundation to a planned expansion. In God's providence, He blessed me with a season of unemployment, allowing me the time to write more than half of what I originally intended to write. When He blessed me again with employment, I realized, with disappointment, that it could be years before I finished the book. Then my new friend, Gary Duff, introduced an idea to me that resulted in the publication of this present work. Gary brought to my attention the idea of utilizing a self-publishing option (at the time I was considering traditional publishers). As I came to appreciate the relative simplicity of the self-publishing route, the idea occurred to me that I could publish what I had already written and hold the remaining content for a later publication. What I had written, I realized, was a coherent whole that was foundational to the remaining things I intended to write. With publishing what I had written, the important message of multigenerational families could be distributed to the church much sooner.

The present book, therefore, addresses the foundational theology of multigenerational families as well as the subjects related to family governance issues. In a future, expanded edition, we will address the subjects of family discipleship, family wealth building, and a host of other relevant subjects, such as transitioning to a clan in later generations and the possibility of generational improvement. The final chapter of the present volume will outline what is expected to be covered in more detail in this anticipated release.

Chapter Summaries

Chapter 1 – The Multigenerational Covenant Family: The first chapter begins by laying out the hermeneutical assumptions behind the argument for the Christian multigenerational family. This section establishes the biblical foundation of the book's arguments, as well as addressing potential skeptics who may not see the validity of the Old Testament's applicability for family life.

From sociologist Carle Zimmerman's work, I then discuss the main models of family that have been operative throughout human history – the trustee family, the domestic family, and the atomistic family. I explain how the Christian family is most like the trustee family, but introduce the term, *covenant family*, as the model of family used in the book.

The next section explains what is meant by the term, *covenant*, as this is not a well-understood concept in the church today and it is vital for understanding the biblical nature of the Christian family. The chapter then proceeds to catalogue the key Scriptural passages that speak to the reality of the multigenerational family. Brief explanatory comments are provided for most of the passages.

The first chapter closes with an extended definition, or summary outline of what a Christian Multigenerational Family is. Key components include the concept of cultural transmission, the covenantal foundation, and dominion as the mission of the family.

Chapter 2 – The Multigenerational Family Blueprint: In this chapter, the different pieces of a multigenerational family plan are introduced. I start with unpacking the maxim that effective governance is the key to a family's ability to successfully transmit its mission over several generations.

Next, the many structural components of a multigenerational family plan are listed (e.g., values, mission, constitution, family "balance sheet," governance policy, discipleship plan, economic stewardship plan, etc.). It is then discussed why most of these structural components will eventually find their way into a family constitution. I also provide how our family defines some of these key structural components (like *constitution* and *family culture*).

Two sample family constitutions are given. This is helpful for families to see similarities and differences in how this governance tool may look. It provides a template from which they can begin their own work.

The chapter concludes on the subject of what I call the *family documents portfolio*. Mature multigenerational families will have the need for a variety of formal policies documented. The portfolio concept helps families organize these different tools.

Introduction

Chapter 3 – The Family Mission: This chapter explains why the experts on multigenerational families uniformly agree that discovering, determining, and codifying a family's mission is the first step necessary to preserve a family's wealth for multiple generations.

The basic pieces of a mission statement are introduced – beliefs, values, vision and the mission itself. Before those traditional pieces are explained, I return to the concept of the covenant to show how a uniquely Christian mission statement is covenantal in nature. Following this, I explain the distinctions between statements of belief, statements of values, and vision statements.

The next section discusses considerations families need to think about before the process of drafting their mission statements. Those considerations include: 1) Is there a common mission for all Christian families, or does each family have a unique mission? 2) Does a family *discover* their mission or creatively *determine* their mission? 3) What "level" of the family should draft the multigenerational mission – the nuclear family (father with mother)? or the extended family (adult siblings with parents)? 4) Similar to the previous question, to which "level" of a family does a multigenerational mission apply – Nuclear? Extended? Multigenerational? 5) Should a family mission be limited to a season, or be generationally permanent, and should it change over time?

Next, the steps to actually draft the mission statement are outlined. Sample family mission statements are then provided. Finally, a section on peripheral elements of mission statements is included – objectives, strategy, tactics, and family aspirations.

Chapter 4 – The Family "Assets and Balance Sheet": This is one of the shorter chapters. I found it did not fit neatly into one of the other chapters and it has a relatively narrow theme. Families can use the analogy of the balance sheet to evaluate their family's progress towards multigenerational faithfulness over time.

The point that "wealth" (and its cousin terms, *assets, capital*, etc.) is more than material, or an economic attribute, is first established. The axiom that the purpose of material/financial wealth is to serve the growth and preservation of non-economic ("spiritual") wealth is established.

A chart listing possible family assets and liabilities is provided. Assets include such things as a family's intellectual and social capital. It includes health, education, and reputation among many other things. Liabilities include things like the failure of family governance, poor beneficiary/trustee relationships, estate taxes, and no mission statement.

When mature families evaluate these questions on an annual basis, they can more objectively determine if they are making progress on their mission ("shareholder equity," analogically).

Chapter 5 – Family Governance and Succession: This chapter begins with a summary and review of James Hughes Jr.'s philosophy of multigenerational family success. The key axioms are: 1) identifying governance as the art of group decision making (that is, if families are to remain intact over several generations, they need to aim to make slightly better decisions as a group in each successive generation) and 2) that each generation needs to reaffirm the family "social compact" (in Christian terms, this is the family covenant).

Following this, I discuss what is involved in defining what a succession and membership policy looks like in a family's governance rules. The concepts of sphere sovereignty and jurisdiction are then discussed. It is important for extended families to know the scope and boundaries for different family members' roles. The importance of clearly identifying the transition to adulthood is also explained.

Governance options a family must choose from are then introduced. The representative republican model and

Introduction

consensus-based decision making take up the most space here as these are the two most often recommended models, depending on which generational phase a family finds itself in.

In the next section, I share with readers some of the particular governance choices we have made for our family. I make clear that I'm not suggesting families copy what we have done, but rather am explaining these choices to help them make their own choices. Subjects include the first born, daughters, first generation estate and family council, clan governance, and a comparison between a confederated republic and a covenantal aristocracy.

Remaining sections discuss alliances and treaties, a theory of multiple covenant relationships, and the necessity of codifying a family's conflict resolution plan.

* * *

Before we launch into the book, a few more introductory comments need to be made.

Pastors

Church leaders (Ephesians 4:11ff) are the equippers of God's people. As fathers are the covenantal "officer" responsible for the equipping of his family, it stands to reason that one of the primary responsibilities of church leaders is to equip fathers to responsibly equip their families (and not do it directly for them!). Therefore, this book is also written for church leaders to aid them in their ministry of equipping fathers in their congregations.

The Many Meanings of the Term Family

The term *family* can refer to a nuclear family, an extended family, a clan, tribe, or a multigenerational family. Each of these, while related, is distinct. We will explore these distinctions in later chapters. In a book on multigenerational families, it is inevitable that each of these kinds of families will be repeatedly referenced, often simultaneously. It is too cumbersome to always provide the qualifying adjective for every reference (for example, adding "nuclear," or "extended," every time *family* is referenced). As such, it will be incumbent upon the reader to allow the immediate context to determine which meaning is inferred. Sometimes *family* is meant broadly to include all the meanings or a sub-set of them as well – reader beware!

I am but a Vessel

There are inevitably going to be things that I strongly advocate for in this book and things that I assume that will be unacceptable to individual families. I ask that rather than discard the whole message, such families incorporate what is valuable to them in building their multigenerational families while discarding those portions they disagree with. If I had to write a book in which every point would be acceptable to every Christian believer, there would be nothing to write!

In one sense, I wish this book would have been written by a scholar with a full-time schedule to devote to the work. I am but a novice to the vast treasures of Reformed thought (Calvin, Bavinck, Van Til, et al) that ultimately lay beneath this work. It pains me to know that there are relevant insights I'm missing due to my ignorance. If it weren't for the observation that it appears this is how God's providence works sometimes, I may not have attempted this project. It seems God sometimes uses very imperfect tools in history and I am such an imperfect tool.

It is inevitable that in this first work there are numerous failures of insight, hermeneutics, and reasoning. One of my hopes is that this book will flush out constructive critics who

Introduction

will expose my blind spots by pointing these failures out. Together, we can then improve the Church and Family's task of building multigenerational families. It would be quite apropos for a book that discusses generational improvement to look forward to the first revision of this work (as I do)!

Chapter 1

THE MULTIGENERATIONAL COVENANT FAMILY

Hermeneutics for a Theology of the Covenant Family

The norms for the Christian multigenerational family are largely found in the Old Testament, and in the Pentateuch particularly. Many Western evangelical Christians are highly suspicious of the idea that the Old Testament remains a valid source of norms and ethics for believers under the New Covenant. Prior to the nineteenth century, the Church characteristically accepted the present validity of the Old Testament for life and doctrine. I do not doubt that this theological change is one major contribution to the demise of the multigenerational family in contemporary Christian culture. This is not the place to make a full argument for the ongoing validity of the Old Testament for Christian faith and practice for today. What follows are some brief points that I hope may help those who are otherwise critical of this use of the Old Testament.

One classic text in supporting the position of the ongoing validity of the Old Testament is 1 Corinthians 10:11. In reference to events in Israel's history, the text responds saying:

> "Now these things happened to them as an example, but they were written down for our instruction, on whom the end of the ages has come."

This New Testament text is important in that it supports the practice of looking to narrative rather than just indicative sections of the Old Testament for instruction for today. Yes, discernment is required, but the fact is, we need to discern rather than just write off the Old Testament narratives as being only applicable to the ancient Israelites.

Another clue in the New Testament is the fact that its authors frequently quote from Old Testament Scripture and apply them for life in the Church. To establish the practice of paying preachers, in 1 Timothy 5:18, the apostle Paul quotes Deuteronomy 25:4 saying:

> "You shall not muzzle an ox when it treads out the grain."

2 Corinthians 13:1 is another example. Here, Paul cites Deuteronomy 19:15 when he writes:

> "This is the third time I am coming to you. Every charge must be established by the evidence of two or three witnesses."

We couldn't conclude this brief defense of the use of the Old Testament without looking at Jesus' statement in Matthew 5:17-19 where He says this:

"[17]Do not think that I came to abolish the Law or the Prophets; I did not come to abolish but to fulfill. [18]For truly I say to you, until heaven and earth pass away, not the smallest letter or stroke shall pass from the Law until all is accomplished. [19]Whoever then annuls one of the least of these commandments, and teaches others to do the same, shall be called least in the kingdom of heaven; but whoever keeps and teaches them, he shall be called great in the kingdom of heaven..."

Opponents to the present authority of the Old Testament certainly have explanations for passages such as these. For the purposes of this study, however, it is taken as a presupposition that the principles taught in the Old Testament remain valid for today for Christian doctrine and ethics. This is still distinct from the question of hermeneutics, however, and so some brief comments there are in order.

At least the following three interpretive principles will be operative in this study:

First – if the New Covenant has not explicitly modified a principle or command in the Old Testament, the Old Testament principle or command remains valid. At the same time, an Old Testament command or pattern may be modified under the New Covenant into a principle, the application of which is to be adapted to different cultural contexts.

Second – the principle of discerning that which is merely descriptive from that which is truly normative should be observed. This is not unique to the Old Testament, of course, and no interpreter denies this in principle. We are acknowledging the necessity of this task as a standard (even though none of us practice it perfectly).

Third — we will not be trapped by what I call the "explicit word fallacy." Here is what I mean. The biblical theology for a multigenerational, covenant family is not only found in passages that speak directly of these things with such words as *generations*, *covenant*, or even the word *family*. If this were so, we would never be able to receive the full doctrine of the Trinity, for example, which is never identified as such in the Bible. A theology of any subject needs to discern if a passage is discussing the subject regardless of what words or phrases are used. For example, Isaac buying land for wells has enormous implications for principles of family life.

Family Model Alternatives

What we're calling the Christian multigenerational family, or, the biblical covenant family, is a particular model of family. What are the alternatives? We'll look at three sources for answers to this question and provide a contribution of our own.

As mentioned in the Introduction, my friend, and church leader, Jeremy Pryor, first introduced me to the idea of Christian multigenerational families. (Let me say at this point, every aspiring Christian multigenerational family needs to read Jeremy's ebook titled, *ReFamily: A Biblical Blueprint*, available at *www.pathsofreturn.com*. It is an invaluable resource for taking the first steps in transitioning to a Christian multigenerational family platform.) Pryor contrasts what he calls *The Western Family* with *The Classical Family*. The *Western Family* is the individualistic family as is typically practiced by modern Western families, Christians included. According to Pryor, the *Classical Family* is the multigenerational family as typically practiced in most cultures outside of the West and even in the West prior to the last couple hundred years. He goes on to say that the biblical model of the family is a redeemed version of the classical family.

Perhaps the most authoritative categorization of families, from an historical and sociological perspective, comes from sociologist Carle C. Zimmerman, in his book, *Family and Civilization*. Zimmerman's exhaustive study of history led him to see three main types of family structures – the trustee family, the domestic family, and the atomistic family.[4] The trustee family...

> "...is so named because it more or less considers itself as immortal, existing in perpetuity and never being extinguished. As a result, the living members are not *the* family, but merely "trustees", of its blood, rights, property, name, and position for their lifetimes. The family is supposed to have existed and to continue to exist forever, so that the individual is subject to family duties first of all, if the family needs him."[5]

The *domestic* family...

> "...is a middle type, arising out of modifications of the trustee family or being revived by governmental or religious sanctions from the atomistic type. The domestic family is the most common type in this world. It satisfies to some extent the natural desires for freedom from family bonds and for individualism, yet it also preserves sufficient social structure to enable the state or body politic to depend upon it as an aid in government and as a source of the extreme power needed by states in carrying out their functions... This domestic family possesses a certain amount of mobility and freedom and still keeps up the minimum amount of familism necessary for carrying on the society."[6]

The *atomistic* family is so called because...

> "...of the rise of the conception that, as far as is compatible with the successful carrying-on of society, the individual is to be freed of the family bonds, and

the state is to become much more an organization of individuals.

... the atomistic family represents the great individual, measuring individualism in terms of legal and social power and responsibility given the individual.

... the individual is held responsible for himself and he alone is accountable to the state, or through the state to other persons."[7]

It should be noted here that Zimmerman saw the atomistic family taking predominance in Western societies in the eighteenth century, and while it remains the dominate type of family today, he did not expect it could survive through the twenty-first century.

While practicing the descriptive science of sociology, Zimmerman did not refrain from affirming his opinion that the domestic type of family ought to be the normative ideal. This can be seen in his statement quoted above, "this domestic family possesses a certain amount of mobility and freedom and still keeps up the minimum amount of familism necessary for carrying on the society."

Finally, we need to look at R. J. Rushdoony's assessment of Carle Zimmerman's categories. Contrary to Zimmerman's preference for the domestic family, Rushdoony claims that the trustee type *is* the biblical model of family. He says, "the trustee family sees its possessions and its work as an inheritance from the past to be transmitted to the future. The family wealth is thus not for private use but for the family's on-going life."[8] The idea of the family as trustee is an excellent paradigm for Christian families to adopt. Before we continue with this terminology, however, we need to add some important distinctions.

I agree with both Pryor's and Rushdoony's sentiment that the biblical model of the family is much more in the direction of the "classical" or "trustee" type in contrast to the individualistic type. However, without proper qualifications, a rejection of the individualism of today's families can lead to an adoption of an equally erroneous collectivism. Collectivism is not the biblical antidote to individualism. Zimmerman points out that in the trustee type of family, individuality is nearly obliterated. In many cases, clan patriarchs had the right, and even expectation, to sacrifice the lives of individual family members when "needed" for the sake of the perceived greater good of the clan. In trustee family systems, public justice is more often assumed by the clan rather than a true civil authority. Think of the history of bloody clan feuds in the Appalachians of the eastern United States. Obviously, this is not what we want, but we need to recognize that there are problems with unbiblical collectivism just as much as there are with unrestrained individualism.

Reformed Dutch thinkers in the early twentieth century, notably Abraham Kuyper and Herman Doowyeeerd, resurrected a tradition that recognized that God had what they called a Law-Order for everything in His creation, including social groups such as the family. Outside of God's revelation the world only has access to the false dualisms of individualism and collectivism. *As the Triune God, only He holds the secret to the ancient and perennial problem of the One and the Many. Only God can let us know what are the proper boundaries and roles between the group and the individual.* Kuyper called this sphere-sovereignty.

Let me repeat that I am in full agreement with Pryor's and Rushdoony's conception of the biblical family model. I am only adding what might be considered a semantic clarification. Pryor explicitly makes a distinction that the biblical family model is a *redeemed* form of the classical family. This is correct. Rushdoony, commenting on Zimmerman's classification writes:

"This does not mean, however, that a strong family in any society is of necessity congenial to Scripture. Far from it. Pagan family life is rife with presuppositions which are radically alien to the Bible. Community is basic to both the pagan and Biblical family, but the pagan family makes itself ultimate rather than God. Ancestor worship is the logical conclusion of pagan family life."[9]

The terminology for classification that we are suggesting in this work is the Biblical Covenantal Family, or just *covenant family* for short. As we will learn in the following sections, a biblical covenant family is, by definition, a multigenerational family. A multigenerational family is so, precisely because it is covenantal—this is an insight that I think many pro-multigenerational families do not see clearly enough. *Covenant includes succession.*

The Biblical Foundations

Before the idea of *covenant* can have meaning as a qualifier when combined with the word *family*, we must first understand what the covenant is all about. In what follows, to explain the biblical covenant, we will primarily look to Ray S. Sutton's discovery of the five parts of the biblical covenant outlined in his book, *That You May Prosper*. Following this, we will review the key Scriptural passages that speak to the reality of the multigenerational family.

The Covenant

We divide our Bibles according to the *Old Testament* and *New Testament*. *Testament* is a covenantal word. It should surprise us, therefore, that the centrality of the covenant is not central in the minds of Bible-believing Christians today.

To say that the covenant is central to Scripture is almost a tautology. Scripture itself is a covenant document.

Indeed, the Father, Son, and Holy Spirit relate covenantally in eternity. Before time began, the Father and Son made a covenant for the redemption of the Son's bride (Isaiah 49:1-7; Eph. 1:4-5; Titus 1:2). That covenant takes expression in history for the first time with the covenant with creation and Adam (Jeremiah 33:19-26; Genesis 1). It is carried through with Noah, Abraham, Israel, David and on into the New Covenant. The administration of the covenant changes such that there are elements of discontinuity. However, there also abides elements of continuity. Under the New Covenant, the Church is still "Abraham's offspring, heirs according to promise" (Gal. 3:29).

Ray Sutton has pioneered a work in discovering the essential components of the biblical covenant structure. While this covenantal structure can be found throughout Scripture, Sutton has found that the book of Deuteronomy is paradigmatic as a foundation for understanding the covenant structure. He notes that Deuteronomy is to the covenant what Romans is to doctrine.

> "But how do we know Deuteronomy is a covenant? Moses says, 'He declared to you His covenant which He commanded you to perform, that is, the Ten Commandments [Words]' (Deut. 4:13). Deuteronomy is the *second* giving of the Ten Commandments, a 'new' covenant so to speak. Moses says of the book as a whole, 'Keep the words of this covenant to do them, that you may prosper in all that you do' (Deut. 29:9). Deuteronomy is definitely a covenant document."[10]

Studying Deuteronomy, Sutton finds the biblical covenant to follow these five parts: Transcendence, Hierarchy, Ethics, Sanctions, and Continuity:[11]

True Transcendence: a biblical covenant begins with a preamble where God declares His transcendence. This does not mean God is distant, but that He is distinct. It is a declaration of His Lordship; His absolute sovereign authority.

Hierarchy: God establishes a *representative* system through which to govern (in each covenantal institution of church, state, and family). He mediates His judgment on earth through a relationship of human representatives and subordination.

Ethics: This section of the covenant outlines the rules and laws that God's people are to obey. (Sutton adds that these stipulations are the way God's people defeat the enemy. By relating to God in terms of ethical obedience, the enemies fall before His children.)

Sanctions: This is perhaps the most complex section of the covenant. While the term "sanction" typically has a negative connotation, in this context, the sanction is not only for cursing for disobedience but also blessing for obedience. This aspect of the biblical covenant could also be called *ratification*. A ceremony is held in the presence of witnesses where a self-maledictory oath (a curse upon oneself) is taken thereby binding God's people to the terms of the covenant He initiated. The key words to note here are *blessing* and *cursing, ratification, ceremony, oath*, and *witnesses*.

Continuity: this final component of the covenant provides the mechanism for the covenant to be transferred from generation to generation. It is based on the principle of inheritance.

Like all categorizations, it is not to be assumed that these "five points" are the only way to categorize the biblical covenant structure. Other scholars have divided it differently. The sanctions section is the first obvious place where some parts can be divided or have different headings (e.g., ratification vs. sanction?). While we may not be able to determine a definitive categorization, using this model is helpful for understanding the structure of the biblical covenant..

The following adaptation of the five-point covenant model suggested by Gary North is an additional helpful tool:
1. Who's in charge here?
2. To whom do I report?
3. What are the rules?
4. What do I get for obeying or disobeying?
5. Does this outfit have a future?[12]

Another thing to notice is that the different aspects of the covenant are always blending and are interdependent. The sanctions section is based on the standards of the ethics section, for example. Mediating sanctions and continuity provisions always involve God's representatives (hierarchy section).

Since this work seeks to focus on the continuity, or succession aspect of the covenant, it would be good to include Sutton's discussion of how covenantal continuity succeeds or fails.[13] He calls this a process of confirmation. The inheritance promised in the continuity provisions does not come all at once but in stages following faithful action. The first is *covenant renewal*. In Deuteronomy we see God gives His people regular ceremonial meals to observe as signs of ongoing communion. The second element required to preserve continuity is *conquest*. Canaan was promised to the Israelites, but they had to actually take possession of it by conquest. "Covenant renewal is supposed to move out from around the throne of God and into civilization. If it doesn't, the inheritance is lost."[14] The third aspect of confirming the covenant is *discipleship*. The children of God's covenant people must be trained in His covenant law or else the next generation will be lost. A lack of faithfulness in any one of these three areas results in discontinuity, or disinheritance from the covenant.

To compliment Sutton's outline of the structure of the biblical covenant, the following definitions of a biblical covenant will help confirm our understanding:

> "A covenant is an enduring agreement which defines a relationship between two parties involving a solemn, binding obligation specified on the part of at least one of the parties toward the other, made by oath under threat of divine curse, and ratified by a visual ritual."[15]

> " '... the fundamental image behind each of the applications of [the word covenant in the Bible] is the use of familial categories for those who are not bound by ties of natural kinship.' Thus, by a ceremony or (quasi-) legal process, people who are not kin are now bound as tightly as any family relationship. Marriage is the best example of this. A man and woman, who are not previously related, are now bound closer than any other bond of blood or kinship."[16]

> "the covenant is a personal-structural bond which joins the three persons of God in a community of life, and in which man was created to participate."[17]

We have established what the biblical covenant looks like. The next question is whether this applies to families. According to John G. Crawford:

> "The ability to call down and carry out God's judgment and sanctions (blessings and curses) is what makes

an institution covenantal. The only examples given in the Bible that have such authority to invoke God's judgments are the family, church, and state (civil government). All answer to God Himself. They are bound in a legal bond or covenant that is ratified in an oath to Him."[18]

We note that marriage, the foundation of a family, is called a covenant in Scripture (Malachi 2:14; Proverbs 2:17).

Families are covenantal institutions created by God. All five parts of the biblical covenant apply to the family. This book is an in-depth exposition and practical application of the last piece of the covenant applied to families – succession. In the following section we will look at key Scripture passages that discuss the family as it relates to its task of covenant succession.

Key Scripture Passages

This section will be more of a catalogue of Scriptural passages than an exposition of these Scriptures. I want to collect the most relevant passages that reveal the fact and application of the multigenerational model of family. I will provide brief comments for most of the passages, however, the main goal is to lay out the Scriptural foundations in one place. No single theme will be developed here, as later sections of the book will refer to these Scriptures for more specific application.

Having a long catalogue of biblical passages quoted is not normal for a book. However, as the sub-title of this book indicates, I intend for this to be a practical manual and not just a book. I want my and other families to have a resource to go to read a summary of the most relevant passages on the multigenerational family.

It needs to be repeated at this point that the passages included here do not exhaust the Bible's teaching on the multigenerational family. For pedagogical reasons, only the most explicit passages have to be selected. Emphases of some words and phrases will be made to draw attention to a key word or idea. For longer passages, just the chapter and verse reference will be made.

Genesis 1:26-28
26 Then God said, "Let us make man in our image, after our likeness. And let them have dominion over the fish of the sea and over the birds of the heavens and over the livestock and over all the earth and over every creeping thing that creeps on the earth."

27 So God created man in his own image, in the image of God he created him; male and female he created them.

28 And God blessed them. And God said to them, "Be fruitful and multiply and fill the earth and subdue it, and have dominion over the fish of the sea and over the birds of the heavens and over every living thing that moves on the earth."

Genesis 2:18, 24
18 Then the Lord God said, "It is not good that the man should be alone; I will make him a helper fit for him."

24 Therefore a man shall leave his father and his mother and hold fast to his wife, and they shall become one flesh.

We will refer to the commission given to man in Genesis 1:26-28 as the Dominion Mandate ("cultural mandate" is another useful label). As will be developed later, this mandate is the foundational mandate given to families. God gave woman to man to help in this dominion work. When children marry, they start a new covenant family. Ray Sutton explains:

Leaving (*'azab*) implies the termination of a covenant bond, the same Hebrew word being used of apostasy from the covenant. ... The covenant being ended is the parental bond. A new covenant or bond is formed by 'cleaving' (*dabaq*). The parental relationship is temporary and the marital covenant is permanent.[19]

Jeremiah 33:19-21, 25-26
19 The word of the Lord came to Jeremiah:20 "Thus says the Lord: If you can break my covenant with the day and my covenant with the night, so that day and night will not come at their appointed time, 21 then also my covenant with David my servant may be broken, so that he shall not have a son to reign on his throne, and my covenant with the Levitical priests my ministers. ...

25 Thus says the Lord: If I have not established my covenant with day and night and the fixed order of heaven and earth, 26 then I will reject the offspring of Jacob and David my servant and will not choose one of his offspring to rule over the offspring of Abraham, Isaac, and Jacob. For I will restore their fortunes and will have mercy on them."

Genesis 1 and 2 display a covenantal pattern but does not use the word for covenant. Jeremiah 33 takes any ambiguity away from whether or not God made a covenant with creation including Adam (where "adam" = "the man" = representative of all of humanity).

Genesis 9:1, 9
1 And God blessed Noah and his sons and said to them, "Be fruitful and multiply and fill the earth. 9 , I establish my *covenant* with you [Noah] *and your offspring after you.*

Notice that God is making a covenant with a people who are not yet even born! And it is through offspring of a covenant family head.

Peter Gentry and Stephen Wellum in their book, *Kingdom Through Covenant*, show that God is not making a brand new covenant here with Noah, but re-establishes the original covenant made with Adam.[20] Notice the same dominion mandate: "be fruitful and multiply."

Malachi 2:14
The Lord has been a witness between you and the wife of your youth against whom you have dealt treacherously, though she is your companion and your *wife by covenant*.

Proverbs 2:17
"...who forsakes the companion of her youth and forgets the *covenant* of her God;"

These verses establish explicitly what is obvious from other contexts — that marriage is a covenantal relationship. The covenantal marriage relationship is the foundation of the covenantal family.

Genesis 12:1-3
Now the LORD said to Abram, "Go from your country and your kindred and your father's house to the land that I will show you. 2 And I will make of you a great nation, and I will bless you and make your name great, so that you will be a blessing. 3 I will bless those who bless you, and him who dishonors you I will curse, *and in you all the families of the earth shall be blessed*.

Galatians 3:29 reads, "And if you are Christ's, then you are Abraham's offspring, heirs according to promise." We are blessed by being spiritual descendants of Abraham. We are spiritually (covenantally) descendants of Abraham's multigenerational family of faith.

Genesis 17:5-8, 13
No longer shall your name be called Abram, but your name shall be Abraham, for I have made you the father of a multitude of nations. 6 I will make you exceedingly fruitful, and I will make you into nations, and kings shall come from you. 7 And I will establish my covenant between me and you *and your offspring after you throughout their generations for an everlasting covenant,* to be God to you and to *your offspring after you.* 8 And I will give to you *and to your offspring after* you the land of your sojournings, all the land of Canaan, for an everlasting possession, and I will be their God.

13 ...both he who is born in your house and he who is bought with your money, shall surely be circumcised. So shall my covenant be in your flesh an everlasting covenant.

Genesis 18:19
For I have chosen him, that he may *command his children and his household after him* to keep the way of the LORD by doing righteousness and justice, so that the LORD may bring to Abraham what he has promised him.

Genesis 48:5-6, 12-16
5 And now your two sons, who were born to you in the land of Egypt before I came to you in Egypt, are mine; Ephraim and Manasseh shall be mine, as Reuben and Simeon are. 6 And the children that you fathered after them shall be yours. They shall be called by the name of their brothers in their inheritance. ...

12 Then Joseph removed them from his knees, and he bowed himself with his face to the earth. 13 And Joseph took them both, Ephraim in his right hand toward Israel's left hand, and Manasseh in his left hand toward Israel's right hand, and brought them near him. 14 And Israel stretched out his right hand and laid it on the head of Ephraim, who was the younger, and his left hand on the head of Manasseh, crossing his hands (for Manasseh was the firstborn). 15 And he blessed Joseph and said,

"The God before whom my fathers Abraham and Isaac walked, the God who has been my shepherd all my life long to this day, 16 the angel who has redeemed me from all evil, bless the boys; and in them let my name be carried on, and the name of my fathers Abraham and Isaac; and let them grow into a multitude in the midst of the earth."

The Bible assumes that patriarchs can (and should) pass down generational blessings and directives. Neglecting this runs the risk of aborting blessings that our descendants would otherwise receive!

"Let my name be carried on," does not mean, let Jacob's individual identity be carried on, but rather the multigenerational identity and mission God gave to Abraham, Isaac, and Jacob, and by virtue of the principle of covenantal succession, to all their (faithful) descendants.

Exodus 34:6-7
The LORD passed before him and proclaimed, "The LORD, the LORD, a God merciful and gracious, slow to anger, and abounding in steadfast love and faithfulness, 7 *keeping steadfast love for thousands*, forgiving iniquity and transgression and sin, but who will by no means clear the guilty, *visiting the iniquity of the fathers on the children*

and the children's children, to the third and the fourth generation."

Just because Western culture (which most Christians have passively adopted) does not operate on a principle of covenantal representation and succession, does not mean that God does not! Acts 2:38-39 ("the promise is to you and your children") proves this principle of family covenantal succession has not been abrogated in the New Covenant.

Deuteronomy 6:1-9, 20-21

"Now this is the commandment—the statutes and the rules — that the LORD your God commanded me to teach you, that you may do them in the land to which you are going over, to possess it, 2 that you may fear the LORD your God, you and your son and *your son's son*, by keeping all his statutes and his commandments, which I command you, all the days of your life, and that your days may be long. 3 Hear therefore, O Israel, and be careful to do them, that it may go well with you, and that you may multiply greatly, as the LORD, the God of your fathers, has promised you, in a land flowing with milk and honey.

4 "Hear, O Israel: The LORD our God, the LORD is one. 5 You shall love the LORD your God with all your heart and with all your soul and with all your might. 6 And these words that I command you today shall be on your heart. 7 You shall teach them diligently to your children, and shall talk of them when you sit in your house, and when you walk by the way, and when you lie down, and when you rise. 8 You shall bind them as a sign on your hand, and they shall be as frontlets between your eyes. 9 You shall write them on the doorposts of your house and on your gates. ...

20 "When your son asks you in time to come, 'What is the meaning of the testimonies and the statutes and the rules that the LORD our God has commanded you?' 21 then you shall say to your son, 'We were Pharaoh's slaves in Egypt. And the LORD brought us out of Egypt with a mighty hand.

The inclusion of "your son's son" proves that this family covenantal responsibility of discipleship is multigenerational. Fathers do not merely have responsibility to see that their own sons are trained, but that their sons' sons – their grandchildren – are trained (again, this does not necessarily imply direct or exclusive training of grandchildren. A father is responsible to train *his* sons in a manner that *they* will train the next generation in faithfulness). Trained to do what? Trained to pass on covenantal faithfulness to the next generation. Carry this process out and the multigenerational implication is obvious.

Deuteronomy 6 is the biblical fountainhead of family education. It will be exposited in depth in our later volume when family discipleship is discussed in detail.

Deuteronomy 23:2-3; 7-8

2 "No one born of a forbidden union may enter the assembly of the LORD. Even to the tenth generation, none of his descendants may enter the assembly of the LORD.

3 "No Ammonite or Moabite may enter the assembly of the LORD. Even to the tenth generation, none of them may enter the assembly of the LORD forever, ...

7 "You shall not abhor an Edomite, for he is your brother. You shall not abhor an Egyptian, because you were a sojourner in his land. 8 Children born to them in the third generation may enter the assembly of the LORD.

This is another Scripture that reveals that God acts representatively across multiple generations of family.

The following quote from Sutton points to other Scriptural examples of this principle of representation across generations:

> Judgment of entire households serves as a recurring Biblical example. God judged the households of Korah, Dathan, and Abiram for rebelling against Moses' leadership (Nu. 16:32). Achan's family was destroyed. The entire household of Haman was destroyed for his sin against Mordecai and the people of God (Esther 9:1-19). Many other examples could be given. God imposes covenantal discontinuity on households, and not just on individuals.[21]

1 Samuel 2:29; 3:13
Why then do you scorn my sacrifices and my offerings that I commanded for my dwelling, and honor your sons above me by fattening yourselves on the choicest parts of every offering of my people Israel?' ...

And I declare to him that I am about to punish his house forever, for the iniquity that he knew, because his sons were blaspheming God, and he did not restrain them.

This should be sobering to fathers. Eli's posterity (his household) was severely cursed precisely because he did not restrain his sons. That is, he did not practice faithful covenant succession by failing to disciple his sons.
And finally (regarding generational representation),

Hebrews 7:9-10
One might even say that Levi himself, who receives tithes, paid through Abraham, for he was still in the loins of his ancestor when Melchizedek met him.

2 Kings 22:8-23:25

This is the famous story of the Book of the Covenant being found and Josiah's reforms. After discovering and reading of the covenant, Josiah and the people renew the covenant. Following this, the whole of Israelite society is radically reformed. Sutton provides this insightful comment on how returning to covenant faithfulness is relevant for the task of societal transformation in our own day:

> *That You May Prosper* is a book about the covenant: what it is and how it works. It is designed to help create what happened in Josiah's day. Like his time, 'covenant' has been forgotten. Unlike his day, it has not yet been rediscovered. (Yes, a lot of Christians talk 'covenant' and talk 'accountability,' but the doctrine simply has not been discussed in terms of what the Bible actually teaches.) *Covenant is the answer at a time when we stand at the threshold of the death of a culture.*[22] [italics mine]

We should also be reminded that the colonial American Puritans explicitly applied the biblical covenant to their *entire* culture and society. The result was the most godly civilization history has ever known. (If Sutton is correct, and I believe he is, the loss of that godly civilization was due to a failure by the Church to maintain faithfulness to the provisions of covenantal continuity.)

Psalm 78:1-8

Give ear, O my people, to my teaching;
incline your ears to the words of my mouth!
2 I will open my mouth in a parable;
I will utter dark sayings from of old,
3 things that we have heard and known,
that our fathers have told us.
4 We will not hide them from their children,

but tell to the coming generation
the glorious deeds of the LORD, and his might,
and the wonders that he has done.
5 He established a testimony in Jacob
and appointed a law in Israel,
which he commanded our fathers
to teach to their children,
6 *that the next generation might know them,*
the children yet unborn,
and arise and tell them to their children,
7 so that they should set their hope in God
and not forget the works of God,
but keep his commandments;
8 and that they should not be like their fathers,
a stubborn and rebellious generation,
a generation whose heart was not steadfast,
whose spirit was not faithful to God.

Psalm 103:17-18
But the steadfast love of the Lord is from everlasting to everlasting on those who fear him, and his righteousness *to children's children*, to those who keep his *covenant* and remember to do his commandments.

The above Psalms are famous core texts for establishing the fact that God's people are to operate their families on a multigenerational platform.

Psalm 127:3-5
Behold, children are a heritage from the LORD,
the fruit of the womb a reward.
4 Like arrows in the hand of a warrior
are the children of one's youth.
5 Blessed is the man
who fills his quiver with them!

He shall not be put to shame
when he speaks with his enemies in the gate.

Proverbs 17:6
Grandchildren are the crown of the aged,
and the glory of children is their fathers.

Proverbs 19:14
Houses and wealth are inherited from parents ...

Proverbs 13:22
A good man leaves an inheritance to his children's children.

We are often reminded that Proverbs are not imperatives of law. But neither are they meaningless statements! Wisdom tells us that it is a good thing for parents (and grandparents) to accumulate and pass wealth to their descendants.

Jeremiah 29:4-6
4 "Thus says the LORD of hosts, the God of Israel, to all the exiles whom I have sent into exile from Jerusalem to Babylon: 5 Build houses and live in them; plant gardens and eat their produce. 6 Take wives and have sons and daughters; take wives for your sons, and give your daughters in marriage, that they may bear sons and daughters; *multiply there*, and do not decrease.

The multigenerational dominion mandate did not cease when Israel (God's people) was in exile.

Jeremiah 35:5-6, 8, 18-19 (Jonadab's descendants)
Then I [Jeremiah] set before the Rechabites pitchers full of wine, and cups, and I said to them, 'Drink wine.' But they answered, 'We will drink no wine, for Jonadab the son of Rechab, our father, commanded us, 'You shall not drink wine, neither you nor your sons forever.' . . . We

have **obeyed** the voice of Jonadab the son of Rechab, our father, in all that he commanded us, to drink no wine all our days, . . .

. . . to the house of Rechabites Jeremiah said, 'Thus says the LORD of hosts, the God of Israel: Because you have obeyed the command of Jonadab your father and kept all that he commanded you, therefore thus says the LORD of hosts, the God of Israel: Jonadab the son of Rechab shall never lack a man to stand before me.'

Jeremiah spoke this to Jonadab's descendants 250 years after he died! Several points can be gleaned from this story:
(1) Here is an example of a unique component to a multigenerational family mission. This will be developed in the section on discovering a family's mission.
(2) This story is another example of the multigenerational family assumption in the Bible. As stated earlier, we cannot capture every example, however, by now the accumulation of these examples should start conveying the weight of this assertion.
(3) Here is more evidence of the role of patriarchs giving directives to the multigenerational family (qualified by sphere sovereignty, of course).
(4) This affirms the high value and God's overwhelming approval of multigenerational faithfulness – "Jonadab the son of Rechab shall never lack a man to stand before me"!

Mark 7:9-13

9 And he said to them, "You have a fine way of rejecting the commandment of God in order to establish your tradition! 10 For Moses said, 'Honor your father and your mother'; and, 'Whoever reviles father or mother must surely die.' 11 But you say, 'If a man tells his father or his

mother, "Whatever you would have gained from me is Corban"' (that is, given to God)— 12 then you no longer permit him to do anything for his father or mother, 13 thus making void the word of God by your tradition that you have handed down. And many such things you do.

John 19:26-27
26 When Jesus saw his mother and the disciple whom he loved standing nearby, he said to his mother, "Woman, behold, your son!" 27 Then he said to the disciple, "Behold, your mother!" And from that hour the disciple took her to his own home.

Jesus affirms that a primary expression of honoring father and mother is providing for them financially when they need it. Covenantal family life does not end when minor children become adults.

Luke 1:17
17and he will go before him in the spirit and power of Elijah, to turn the hearts of the fathers to the children, and the disobedient to the wisdom of the just, to make ready for the Lord a people prepared."

Malachi 4:5-6
5 "Behold, I will send you Elijah the prophet before the great and awesome day of the LORD comes. 6And he will turn the hearts of fathers to their children and the hearts of children to their fathers, lest I come and strike the land with a decree of utter destruction."

Acts 2:38-39
And Peter said to them, "Repent and be baptized every one of you in the name of Jesus Christ for the forgiveness of your sins, and you will receive the gift of the Holy Spirit.

39 ***For the promise is for you and for your children*** and for all who are far off, everyone whom the Lord our God calls to himself."

Galatians 6:16
And as for all who walk by this rule, peace and mercy be upon them, and upon ***the Israel of God.***

1 Corinthians 7:14
14 For the unbelieving husband is made holy because of his wife, and the unbelieving wife is made holy because of her husband. Otherwise your children would be unclean, but as it is, they are holy.

Galatians 3:29
And if you are Christ's, then you are Abraham's offspring, heirs according to promise.

The above four passages are meant to establish the conclusion that the New Covenant people of God are the recipients of the promise made to Abraham. The covenantal promise is still to "us" *and* "our children."

1 Timothy 5:3-6
3 Honor widows who are truly widows. 4 But if a widow has children or grandchildren, let them first learn to show godliness to their own household and to make some return to their parents, for this is pleasing in the sight of God. 5 She who is truly a widow, left all alone, has set her hope on God and continues in supplications and prayers night and day, 6 but she who is self-indulgent is dead even while she lives. 7 Command these things as well, so that they may be without reproach. 8 ***But if anyone does not provide for his relatives, and especially for members of his household, he has denied the faith and is worse than an unbeliever.***

Economic provision for not only our nuclear family, but extended family as well (should they need it), is apparently at the height of biblical faithfulness! Christians today no longer assume the extended family has an economic identity (distinct from the nuclear family, but nevertheless real). This needs to change.

Defining a Christian Multigenerational Family

Let's start with a provisional definition and then we'll unpack the pieces: A Christian multigenerational family is a family incorporated on the foundation of covenant marriages and covenantal obligations to children, extended over multiple generations, centered around a mission for the family received from God, with the responsibility of preserving, expanding, and most importantly, successfully transmitting that missional-faithfulness to every succeeding generation of the family.

And here is another possible definition: a multigenerational family is a family that exists throughout multiple generations identified by a common covenant that has been faithfully transmitted from generation to generation.

Cultural Transmission

At the heart of what a multigenerational family means, is something I call cultural transmission. You could also call it cultural transfer. Norm Willis, pastor of Christ Church Kirkland, prefers the term generational transfer.[23] The transmission, or transfer, refers to the process of passing a family's culture from one generation to the next.

But why do I use the term "culture"? Because it is the best comprehensive word I can find that encapsulates all the things a family must transfer to their next generation. These are the things that multigenerational families pass on to to their descendants: mission, values, vision, knowledge, skills, family rhythms, assets, and experiences. At the head of this list is mission. All the other pieces can be potentially implied from a family's mission. So, while on the one hand it is more direct to say that a family's primary stewardship is to pass on its mission to the next generation, the concept of a family culture helps communicate that there is a large host of things that a family passes on that are necessary to support that mission.

Why must multigenerational families be so intentional about passing on their mission to succeeding generations? Doesn't it just happen automatically? The answer is that history proves that without such intentionality, a family's culture typically dies after three generations. James Hughes, Jr., author of *Family Wealth: Keeping It In The Family*, writes about this phenomenon and has found that every culture throughout history has had a proverb summarizing this phenomenon.[24] In America, ours is, "shirtsleeves to shirtsleeves in three generations." While the emphasis of these proverbs is on the dissipation of wealth, it applies equally to the entirety of a family's culture as well.

Multigenerational families are about overcoming that entropic law embodied in the shirtsleeves to shirtsleeves proverb. They are about guarding the life of the mission entrusted to them from its certain death should they neglect their stewardship.

Earlier we noted that the trustee family described by sociologist Carle C. Zimmerman had aspects that are commendable on the one hand and other aspects to be avoided. However, the basic idea of a multigenerational family playing the role of a steward-trustee of the historical family's resources is a good perspective. Quoting Rushdoony again: "the trustee family sees its possessions and its work as an inheritance from the past to be transmitted to the future.

The family wealth is thus not for private use but for the family's on-going life."[25]

Covenant Foundation

People often mistakenly assume that blood ties are the foundational bond of families. The marriage relationship should remove this assumption right away. Recall one of the definitions for covenant given earlier that explained that a covenant takes two parties who are not family and makes them closer than any naturally existing family blood ties. The reality of the covenantal relationship of the family also establishes the fact that adopted children are just as much children as biologically born children.

Applying the five parts of the covenant, we can say the biblical family should be characterized by the following:

A covenant family confesses Jesus Christ as Lord (*transcendence*). God has sovereignly taken hold of the family for Himself and has put His Spirit into them such that their whole lives proclaim, "as for me and my house, we will serve the LORD."

A covenant family is one where the father is head of the household, not merely in name, but in substance (*hierarchy*). The father has the ultimate responsibility to be the family's teacher-discipler (prophet), worship leader (priest) and dominion governor (king). The father represents the family before God and the world. (Yes, in the absence of a father, the mother necessarily fills this role. As in all exceptions to rules, the exception does not obliterate the rule.)

A covenant family is one in which the entire Word of God is the standard for the family's life (*ethics*). Again, this is not merely lip service. The family characteristically studies the Scriptures and progressively conforms its life to the standard of the Word of God.

A covenant family is founded on a covenant marriage between believers (*ratification*). For a spouse who converted after marriage, his or her profession and baptism provide the covenantal foundation for their children (1 Cor. 7:14). The family seeks to see their children baptized (whether as professing believers or infants). The family (representationally through the parents, at least) regularly participates in the Lord's Supper communion with a local congregation.

A covenant family disciples their children to steward the gospel so as to successfully transmit the Dominion-Commission task to the next generation (*succession*).

Dominion is the Mission

The mission of the covenantal-multigenerational family is, in a word, dominion (Genesis 1:26-28). In a later chapter on discovering the family mission, we will demonstrate how the Great Commission of Matthew 28 is, in part, a New Covenant manifestation of the original Dominion Mandate. While each family will have unique elements to their mission (rooted in God's love of diversity), for Christian families, that mission is rooted in these four, inter-related, Scriptural fountainheads: 1) The Dominion Mandate, 2) The Abrahamic Covenant, 3) The Kingdom of God, and 4) The Great Commission.

Four Components of Christian Multigenerational Families

Another way of summarizing the multigenerational family is to see it consisting of these four components:
- A *Culture*
- A *Discipleship Curriculum*
- Characterized by a principle of *Reproduction*, and
- Possession of *Tools* to support multigenerational faithfulness

The culture of a family was introduced above. At its heart is a mission, and surrounding that mission are first values, and then things like knowledge, skills, traditions, assets, and tools.

A discipleship curriculum can go by other names like "training program" or "educational plan," but for Christian families I prefer to emphasize that the concept of discipleship be at the heart of a family's educational and training plans. The discipleship curriculum is the mechanism a family uses to train the current generation in the family mission.

Reproduction is the nature of multigenerational families in three aspects. First, families seek to reproduce the culture and mission of the family in the current, living generation. Second, they reproduce biologically (or by adoption). There's no family to pass a mission on to without new children! And finally, they reproduce generationally. They seek that their mission will be entrusted and enlarged to generations they will never see (at least this side of glory).

Tools include all those things that assist in the family mission. Raw assets are tools. Governance documents for sibling and cousin generations are tools. Legal and financial agreements and programs are tools. Strategic family retreats are tools. A generational family on mission will seek to grow their tools, not for the tools' sake, but for the mission's sake.

Each of these different components will be elaborated in detail in the chapters that follow.

Chapter 2

THE MULTIGENERATIONAL FAMILY BLUEPRINT

We are about to enter into a potentially complex subject – outlining all the structural components of a multigenerational family and how those pieces relate to each other. One difficulty is that each piece is organically related to all the other pieces, such that talking about one does not make full sense without understanding the other pieces. The dilemma, of course, is that it is difficult to explain everything all at once. We've already been introduced to many of the key pieces (mission, generational transmission, etc.) but it is time to get specific and technical. And then there is the question of "where to start?" There are multiple options for entry points. I'm persuaded that the idea of governance is a good place to launch from.

James Hughes Jr. is a leading authority on multigenerational family practices, helping wealthy families with succession for over three decades. He has found that the leading criteria that determines whether a family will successfully transmit its wealth – financial and spiritual – over multiple generations is the quality of their governance system. He writes:

Successful long-term wealth preservation requires the creation and maintenance of a system of governance or joint decision making, to the end of making slightly more positive decisions than negative ones over a period of at least one hundred years.[26]

It is not necessarily intuitive that the issue of governance is the key element that determines the probability of success for a family's multigenerational longevity, but historical analysis proves that it is. If we are serious about building a multigenerational family, do we have any basis for assuming we can ignore this universal consensus among the authorities?

To speak of family discipleship as the "key" to multigenerational faithfulness may seem more intuitive. And in one sense you would be right. Family discipleship is the *heart* of covenantal succession. However, if that family discipleship is not connected to the tools of generational succession, any quality of discipleship produced in a single generation will dissipate in a generation or two. Also, family discipleship that is formed by a beginning, pioneer generation is, by definition, inferior to a family discipleship culture that has had generations to mature. Tie effective family discipleship to effective generational governance systems and you have a recipe that will make our enemy quiver!

As alluded to in Hughes' quote above, the essential element of governance is a system of group decision making. A family that improves its group decision-making process (governance) improves its ability to transmit itself further into the future.

From this insight into governance flows certain inevitable implications. All those who contemplate this issue for any length of time realize that families desiring multigenerational continuity at some point must determine and express their governance philosophy in a mission statement and constitution, at a minimum. These are the foundational governance tools.

Expressing your family's mission and governance system can take several forms. Understanding the distinction between the different pieces of what I'm calling the *structural components* (or a blueprint) of a multigenerational family and their relationships to each other is more important than the form these things take. With that said, let me list those different components now and then we can start discussing the nature and relationship among them (and remember this is just one way to make this list; dozens of alternate labels could be used and shorter or longer lists could be created):

- Beliefs
- Values
- Covenant
- Mission
- Vision
- Constitution
- Family Documents Portfolio
- The Five "Levels" of the Family
- Family Culture
- Aspirations
- Initiatives
- Family Assets and "Balance Sheet"
- Governance Policy
- Succession Policy
- Family Discipleship Plan
- Economic Stewardship Plan
- Roles

Most of the above components should eventually find their way into a written document. Whether you split them up into several documents or consolidate them into as few as possible is up to your family. Lee Hausner and Douglas Freeman in their book, *The Legacy Family*, for example, suggest drafting what they call *The Strategic Plan* (which consists primarily of the family mission) separately from the family constitution.[27] For my family, I have chosen to include the family mission statement as part of the constitution.

Don't get overwhelmed with the amount of work this project entails. Take the long-term view. You'll spend your lifetime tweaking these things anyway. Prioritize and just start working.

Your family will need to decide for itself how it is going to define what it means by mission, covenant, constitution, culture, and even the word *family* itself. To help you begin thinking about these things, in what follows I have provided the definitions and distinctions our family made regarding these ideas:

Constitution. The family constitution is the codified repository of a family's multigenerational plan and policies; it serves as a guide to family decision making. The purpose of the Family Constitution is to serve the multigenerational task of transmitting the *family's culture* down the generations. The codifying process helps parents recall decisions made and their reasons. It serves as a reference tool when the growing volume of content and its complexity becomes too difficult to manage on the basis of the parents' memory alone. It becomes a record of the maturing evolution of a family's understanding and practice of multigenerational faithfulness. For a family's descendants to improve upon its forbearers' practices, it needs to understand the history of the evolution of those practices.

Covenant and Mission. The relationship between the terms *Covenant* and *Mission* needs to be understood. Limiting the family agreement (compact) to the language of *mission* suggests the agreement is only between family members. Whenever men make an agreement with God, however, that is properly called a covenant. We came to recognize that at the heart of the purpose of the Multigenerational

Family is an agreement, or a promise, with our God. Therefore, at the most foundational level, the family constitution and the family mission statement is a covenant—a family covenant with our God. That covenant is secondarily expressed in terms of a mission. At times it is more useful to speak in terms of *covenant* on the one hand or of *mission* in other contexts. But it should be noted these ideas are at the same time distinct and overlapping.

Covenant and *Constitution*. Another relationship that needs to be made clear is the relationship between the term *Covenant* and *Constitution*. The Covenant is the heart of the Constitution. The Constitution is broader than the Covenant in its purpose of establishing secondary policies, rules, and procedures, among other things. At times, however, we reference the Constitution with the intention of focusing on its heart—the Covenant.

To summarize the above, language compels us to make use of multiple terms, and the reader should be aware that there is a high degree of overlap between the terms *family mission, family covenant, family constitution* and *family culture* (also, recall our earlier explanation of the terms *family culture* and the different levels of *family* itself).

We should also introduce the biblical term, *household*, at this point. First of all, when the Bible uses the term "family," it is more often than not talking about what we would call the extended family. That is, perhaps, the Bible's default assumption of the primary level of family over against our Western assumption of the nuclear family being the primary level. And in contrast to the Western conception of the nuclear family, the biblical *household* included bondservants living with the family and perhaps even adult children of the head of the family, if they still lived with the family. We will discuss jurisdictional distinctions between parents and adult children later; for now, it is important to note that biblical notions of family have a smaller overlap with our modern conceptions than we might suppose.

This will be elaborated in more depth in the chapter on governance. However, a word regarding the relationship between a family constitution and the different levels of a family is in order here at the outset. First, regarding the governance aspects of a family constitution, it is more applicable to an extended family (and clan and tribe, if your multigenerational family matures to this point). Remember that governance is about the rules for group decision making. A nuclear family already has a governance structure made sufficiently clear from Scripture. A husband and father is head of his household with his wife as "chief advisor." A multigenerational family is something that exists throughout time. Only living generations who steward this "invisible" thing called a multigenerational family can act governmentally. There is a wonderfully mysterious relationship among the nuclear, extended, and multigenerational families!

Sample Outlines of a Family Constitution

Our family chose to use the constitution format as the overall plan for our multigenerational family. Others (e.g., Hausner & Freeman, *The Legacy Family*) use the constitution for governance questions only and have a separate document that addresses what might be called a family strategic plan. This might be advisable for young families who want to defer governance questions for their extended family for later. For our family, however, rather than simply mirroring a civil constitution, we recognized that a *family* constitution should tend in the direction toward a biblical covenant structure, which is going to include more than just governance questions (e.g., historical preambles). In other words, the idea of a comprehensive, multigenerational *plan* is appropriate.

Here is the current outline of our family constitution:
I. INTRODUCTION
    a. Versions of the Family Constitution
    b. Defining Terms
    c. The Family Documents Portfolio
    d. Family History

II. FAMILY COVENANT AND MISSION
    a. Core Values and Beliefs
        i. Statement of Faith
    b. Covenant and Mission
        i. Explanation of Mission Components
    c. Vision
    d. Reputation Aspirations

III. SUCCESSION AND GOVERNANCE
    a. Succession Policy
        i. Introduction
        ii. Patriarchy and the Firstborn
        iii. Initial Succession
        iv. Nuclear Family Constitutions and Multigenerational Family Constitution
        v. The Family Estate
        vi. Clan Triggering Event
        vii. Multiple Covenants and Multiple Estates
        viii. Extended Family Estates
    b. Governance Policy
        i. Membership
        ii. Principle of Decentralized Authority
        iii. The Family Council
        iv. The Clan as Confederated Republic
        v. The Legislative Branch – The Clan Congress
        vi. The Executive Branch
        vii. The Judicial Branch
        viii. Alliances and Treaties

IV. ESTATE PLAN
    a. Foundation of Core Assets: Human and Spiritual

      b. Enterprising Producers Before Investors
      c. Austrian Economics and the Alpha Strategy
      d. Quality Income Securities
      e. Wealth Cycle Investing
      f. Groom an Investing Expert
      g. The Family Bank
      h. Off-Shore Perpetual Trust
      i. International Diversification
      j. Distribution of the Family Estate
V. TRAINING PLAN
      a. Curriculum Overview
      b. Faith Training
      c. Family Rhythms
      d. Liberal Arts Training
      e. Family Mission Training
      f. Business and Financial Training
      g. Manual Skills
      h. Experiential Opportunities and Events
VI. ROLES
      a. Family Roles
      b. Experts
VII. MEMBER SIGNATURES

The following is a sample family constitution provided by Lee Hausner and Douglas Freeman in their book, *The Legacy Family:*[1]

I. PURPOSE OF THE FAMILY CONSTITUTION
II. DEFINITIONS
      a. Constitution or Family Constitution
      b. Family Group
      c. Family Member
      d. Incapacity
      e. Issue
      f. Majority Vote
      g. Member or Members

    h. Quorum
    i. Senior Generation
    j. Shared Asset or Shared Assets
    k. Spouse
    l. Super-Majority
    m. Unanimous Vote
III. FAMILY GOVERNANCE
    a. Family Council
    b. Election
    c. Tenure
    d. Responsibilities and Authority
    e. Compensation
    f. Alternates
    g. Leadership Roles
IV. SHARED ASSETS
V. FAMILY COMMUNICATION
    a. Reporting on Shared Assets
    b. Family Meetings
    c. Family Retreats
VI. CODE OF CONDUCT
VII. CONFLICT RESOLUTION
    a. Informal Process
    b. Formal Process
    c. Third Party Intervention
VIII. REVIEW, ASSESSMENT, AND MODIFICATION OF FAMILY CONSTITUTION
    a. Statement of Values
    b. Review Process
    c. Third Party Review
    d. Assessment of Benchmarks and Milestones
    e. Process
    f. Amendment Procedures
IX. ADOPTION [ratification]

As you can tell from looking at the two family constitution outlines above, there are different ways to structure your constitution, and at the same time you should notice that there are principles and themes that should be common to all family constitutions as well.

Family Documents Portfolio

The Family Constitution is not the only vital document of a multigenerational family. Like a political constitution, it paints the broad macrostructure of a family's multigenerational plan. Certain aspects of a family's vision, policies and plans are better recorded in separate documents due to their own length, complexity, and specificity. For example, while the constitution will address the high level view of a family's child education plan and the family's estate plan, separate documents covering the details of those plans will exist.

We have established a Family Documents Portfolio, which is the collection of all these vital documents. Examples of other documents that may be in this portfolio include: the family discipleship plan, family member resumes (these are more necessary as the second generation matures), the family genealogy, and actual legal contracts when they come about such as, trusts, family business incorporation documents, and common investment contracts.

Again, your family documents portfolio will be unique to your family, but to help give you some ideas, the following is a description of our current Family Documents Portfolio:
- Child Educational Vision
- Child Discipline & Training System
- Family Genealogy
- Family Initiatives Summary (see below for explanation)
- Commentary Papers (see below for explanation)
- Appendix Papers (see below for explanation)

Family Initiatives Summary: the Multigenerational Family Mission is expected to be enduring in perpetuity down the generations (apart from modifications from an increase in the family's discernment and wisdom where it is determined it should be changed). However, there are secondary mission objectives that serve the larger family mission that are temporary goals. An example of such a goal might be the purchase of a farm or the sending of a family member to learn a skill. Those secondary goals will be called Family Initiatives and will be summarized in a separate document titled, Family Initiatives Summary.

Commentary Papers: The Constitution is intended to be as concise as possible on the essential elements of the family's multigenerational purposes and plans. Brief explanatory comments can be relegated to footnotes within the Constitution. Some subjects, however, need extended explanation and are better located outside of the main text of the Constitution. These will be referred to as *Commentary Papers*. A perfect example would be a paper explaining the family's beliefs about the Kingdom of God. The Kingdom of God is obviously highly relevant to our family mission. However, this subject is not uniformly understood by the broader Church and would take several pages of exposition. This is better placed outside of the Constitution itself.

Appendix Papers: Long-term content is to be incorporated into the main body of The Family Constitution. Temporary, or new and provisional, content can be stored as an *Appendix* item that may later be incorporated into the main body if and when it warrants it.

It is important that you keep good records of all your family documents. I'll repeat this again, if all this seems like unnecessary complications, that is only because your mind has drifted back into thinking of a single, terminal generation. Imagine, once again, a mature, multigenerational family operating as a clan in the sixth generation. You are talking about potentially thousands of family members working together. It is impossible for such a group to operate without detailed plans and careful documentation. I am encouraging pioneer generations to lay the necessary groundwork.

In the chapters that follow, you will notice they follow closely to the outline of the family constitution. That is as it should be, since after all, it provides the structure for the comprehensive multigenerational family plan. We are now ready to dive into the details beginning with the family mission statement.

Chapter 3

THE FAMILY MISSION

Mission statements are more commonly associated with an activity of businesses. Secondarily, most of us, at one time or another, have been encouraged to write a *personal* mission statement. It is not as common to hear about drafting a family mission statement. This is probably due to at least two factors. First, we might assume that mission statements are in fact primarily associated with businesses (or other organizations) and then couple that with an assumption that since families are not businesses, they should not act like businesses.

The second reason why family mission statements are more rare is simply due to the influence of modern, Western individualism. Today, the idea of a family "on mission" feels out of place, while speaking of an individual's "passion," "dreams," and "goals," are commonplace. For the ancients, the exact opposite would be true. I have already argued earlier why I think this default cultural assumption should not be held by Christian families.

As for the "families are not businesses" critique, while there is a kernel of truth there, there is also a hidden falsehood. Certainly, the modern business corporation is a different beast than the family (CEO, board of directors, profit motive, etc.). However, in biblical times (and most other ages) the family was also the center of economic productivity in society. There was not a separation of family and "business." James Hughes Jr. writes:

> "A family's ability to remain in business over a long-period of time always comes down to excellent long-term succession planning, regardless of how successful the family is financially.
>
> "Families attempting long-term wealth preservation often don't understand that they *are* businesses and that the techniques of long-term succession planning practiced by all other businesses are available to them as well. A family that starts its long-term wealth preservation planning by adopting the metaphor that it is a business will begin with a wonderful psychological tool."[1]

In the past, multigenerational families were on mission long before the modern corporation came onto the scene and before Western individualism stole this missional heart from families. While families are not to be equated with businesses, in a much greater respect, as James Hughes says, they should think of themselves more like a business in terms of its multigenerational and institutional nature. And as I mentioned earlier, all families already have a mission even if they are not aware of it at the conscious level. We are just encouraging families to be more intentional with their mission.

The literature on mission statements reveal they come in different sizes and flavors. For our purposes, in this chapter we will focus on the following typical components: beliefs, values, vision, and the mission itself (which may or may not include things like strategy and objectives). While not as common, I will also be speaking of covenant, aspirations, and initiatives.

One of the differing perspectives in the literature is where to begin. Do you begin with a mission statement or a vision statement? Or do you start with beliefs and values? While I have found that there is a more logical order of relationship among these components, there may be more strategic entry points when a family begins this work. For example, beliefs and values logically precede mission since a mission is but an expression of one's beliefs and values. However, it is much more satisfying to begin working on a mission statement than a values statement and that psychological motivation may be a strategic benefit. There are many entry points (values? vision? mission?) and it seems families are free to enter at any point that makes the most sense for them. When the work is done, all pieces will be addressed.

I will say this one more time. All individuals and groups have values, beliefs, a mission, a vision, strategies, and objectives. But most of these groups hold these things at a subconscious level. That is, they are not consciously aware of them.

When individuals or groups want to become more effective, they must seek to understand each of these components. In the process of discovery, they may find contradictions. For the sake of integrity, they will then be forced to change one or more of these components.

For multigenerational families to be effective (that is, pass on their family mission and culture for generations), they too must grow in understanding their beliefs, values, vision, mission, and strategies and improve upon them.

Before we launch into the subject of beliefs and values, we need to address the subject of covenant.

Covenant

Earlier, we made the statement that the concept of a Christian family's mission overlaps with the concept of covenant. When I first began studying multigenerational families, the experts uniformly talked about family mission statements. These experts, however, were writing from a secular perspective. Over time, my biblical studies revealed that a specifically *Christian* mission statement is covenantal by nature. This is a book about *Christian* multigenerational families. The qualifying term *Christian*, by definition, links a family to Christ, who is their covenantal head. Mission is about accomplishing an objective for a specific purpose. A Christian family is not on mission for any 'ol purpose it fancies. It is on mission *for* Christ according to His terms or else it is no *Christian* mission at all.

A Christian covenant is a *responsive* (God initiates) *promise* of *faithfulness* to God. While your family may use the language of mission, do not forget that underneath that, the nature and substance of your mission is that of a covenant–a promise to God to be faithful to Him in the specific way He reveals to your family. And remember, covenants have stipulations–blessings and curses. This is serious business. Proceed in reverent fear AND in bold freedom in the knowledge of our access to the throne of God by grace.

Beliefs and Values

While I recommend families begin working directly on their mission statements first (for motivational reasons, if for nothing else), beliefs and values underlie everything else and so we are going to talk about them first.

Beliefs and values are similar in that most value statements could also be belief statements. For this reason, organizations usually have just one section dedicated to their core beliefs and values and it is usually labeled as their Values Statement. While the two are similar, it is good to acknowledge the distinction. B*eliefs* have to do with *truth* and *falsity*–what is considered true versus what is considered false.

Values have to do with what is believed to be *good* or *bad*, *better* or *worse*.

Note the following two statements. While they can be categorized as belief statements (they can be true or false) they are more specifically addressing the question of value – what is good, or what is better: "*Knowledge and skills are the keys to success.*" "*Give a man bread and feed him for a day, but teach him to fish and feed him for life*". These example *maxims* may set the *missional* priorities of self-sufficiency over consumeristic dependency. Expressed in terms of a value statement it might look like this: "We promote a spirit of independence and service over dependency and consumption."

Here are a few examples of value statements that might find their way into a Christian family mission statement (conceptually add the statement, "we believe ..." before each):
- The glory of God is the highest human aim.
- Maturity is most evidenced in comprehensive fruitfulness.
- Stewardship of family as God's tool in His Kingdom expressed through educational formation of family members becoming of effective royal sons and daughters in God's kingdom.

And here are a few examples of belief statements that might find their way into a Christian family mission statement:
- Jesus Christ is Lord.
- There is one God, Creator of all things.
- Justification is per the Reformation mottos — of Christ alone, by grace alone, through faith alone.

For drafting your family's beliefs, I recommend thinking in terms of a statement of faith – that is, what you would expect from a local church. The balancing act of statements of faith is to be broad enough to allow endorsement by all those intended to be included by not incorporating truly secondary points that are highly debatable, while at the same time specific enough to be meaningful. You may also consider referencing a historic confession such as the Apostles and Nicene Creeds, the Westminster Confession, or London Baptist Confession (with any modifications as necessary).

The Family Vision Statement

> "A vision statement outlines what an organization wants to be, or how it wants the world in which it operates to be (an "idealized" view of the world). It is a long-term view and concentrates on the future. It can be emotive and is a source of inspiration. For example, a charity working with the poor might have a vision statement which reads, 'A World without Poverty.'"[2]

> "Many people mistake the vision statement for the mission statement, and sometimes one is simply used as a longer term version of the other. However they are distinct; with the vision being a descriptive picture of a desired future state; and the mission being a statement of purpose and action, applicable now as well as in the future. The mission is therefore the means of successfully achieving the vision."[3]

As can be inferred from the above two statements, it is most common to understand the vision of an organization as conceptually prior to its mission ("the mission is therefore the means of successfully achieving the vision"). A family vision statement is the desired ideal picture of what you hope your family will look like in the future and what its impact will be.

To begin working on this, the first obvious question is what time frame are you going to use? fifty years? 100 years? 200 years? Like many other details, there is not a "right answer" to this question and will be a choice you will have to make for your family. At the same time, there are better timeframes than others (ten years is meaningless from a multigenerational standpoint, and 2,000 years is too abstract). You can also elect to describe multiple timeframes. Our family has elected a 100-year window. It is out of reach of a single generation and therefore pulls us in the multigenerational direction, but is also not too far out such that we expect to see whether our actions in this generation will bear fruit in the next generation.

Here are some categories to consider in drafting your family vision statement:

- How large is the family (clan?)?
- What is the financial condition of the family/clan?
- What kind of Kingdom impact is the clan making in the world?
- What is your family's reputation?
- What are positive traits characterized by most individual families within the clan?
- What resources are available to the family?
- What are the family accomplishments?

Considerations Before Drafting the Family Mission Statement

We have come to what is perhaps the heart of what transitions a family from a terminal-generation family to a full-orbed, biblical multigenerational family – the drafting of a multigenerational family mission statement. As noted earlier, while there are many assumptions that precede bringing a family's mission to conscious awareness, drafting this statement is typically the first multigenerational project a family undertakes in making this transition.

Before we discuss some recommended steps for drafting your family mission statement, we first need to answer a few foundational questions that are inherently wrapped up with

the subject of a Christian multigenerational family mission. Those questions include:
- Is there a common mission for all Christian families, or does each family have a unique mission? The short answer is both/and.
- Does a family *discover* their mission or creatively *determine* their mission? Again, the short answer is both/and.
- What "level" of the family should draft the multigenerational mission – the nuclear family (father with mother)? Or the extended family (adult siblings with parents)?
- Similar to the above question, to which "level" of a family does a multigenerational mission apply – Nuclear? Extended? Multigenerational?
- Should a family mission be limited to a season, or be generationally permanent, and should it change over time?

Those last three questions are all inter-related and may be foundational to the others, so we will discuss those first.

Recall this is a book about *multigenerational* families. It is certainly possible for parents to draft a family mission statement that is applicable only to their nuclear family and their minor children. Better that than nothing. But assuming a multigenerational perspective, how do a father and mother "speak for" descendants they will never see?

The authors writing on the subject of multigenerational families (Hughes, Hausner and Freeman, Bonner, et. al.) assume they are speaking to families of wealth where a founding father who built the wealth is now in his senior years and is beginning to draft a multigenerational family mission with his adult children. These authors uniformly advise that the second generation of adult siblings have substantial, if not equal, input to the creation of the family mission as their parents. They found the principle of ownership applies – people are generally vested in something proportional to the degree of their creative ownership.

I affirm this principle of ownership in the second (and subsequent) generation and I will say more about it below. However, first I need to remind readers what is unique about specifically *Christian* families. Wealthy families typically start with the question of how to preserve the family wealth generationally, and then find out they need to hold "spiritual" values in common to preserve their wealth over several generations. Christian families know they have a covenantal obligation to transmit their culture of faith and its mission down the generations and subsequently "find out" they will need to add the growth and preservation of material wealth to successfully support that generational ("spiritual") mission.

In other words, even poor, let alone middle class, Christian families in the first generation need to begin building their multigenerational families.

Let's take a look at an insightful quote from Jeremy Pryor on this subject to help us make progress resolving these questions:

> "The concept of a family vision can be short-term, something you feel called to for a season, long-term, something you feel called to for life, or multi-generational, something your children and grandchildren feel called to. The longer the scope of the vision the more it's important to allow God to place the calling on your kids' hearts. A calling may span the generations by going to just one or a small number of your children, while the others receive other callings the family must also affirm and support. It's generally helpful for parents to begin to craft at least a short-term description of their vision to give their efforts focus and to communicate to their family and their community the

direction they feel God is leading them. As you walk more into your seasonal vision God will often begin to show you if the scope is bigger than what you originally conceived."[4]

You can see from Pryor's quote here that the multigenerational family mission is something dynamic. This is also a "both/and" thing. There is a place for *fathering* a multigenerational family vision as well as a place for subsequent generations to take creative ownership of a multigenerational vision.

While there is place for both first and second generation input into a family mission, given our modern preoccupation with individualism, the fathering role in multigenerational discipleship needs to be emphasized. Norm Willis in his book, *The Ancient Path*, has captured the critical fathering principle in generational transfer. Several extended quotes will serve us well in establishing this biblical reality:

Life in the Kingdom of God is found in succession, which has a two-step process:
- Receiving the heart of a father.
- Passing your heart on to a son.[5]

Often I hear parents and children who say that at eighteen you must go out and find your own way. The underlying shame behind that philosophy is the former way they were following, namely their parents' way, was wrong. If their parents' way were right, there would be no need to find an alternative way. As parents with a vision of generational transfer, we must not fall into this deception of modernity. The way for our children to follow, whether they are eighteen or eighty-four, is the way of the Kingdom of God.[6]

Many dreams are lost because they were never passed to the second generation. Dreams of an eternal nature are conceived by one generation and built by another.

... Destiny is a cycle of conceiving and building. One generation conceives; the next generation builds.

... How many frustrated ministries do we have in Christendom today because they are either trying to build when they were only to conceive, or they are trying to conceive when they were ordained to build? Yes, the sovereignty of God can ordain for one generation to do both, but usually the Lord chooses one generation to conceive it and another generation to build it. Our responsibility is to discern our position before God and not presume we are to just conceive, just build or even do both.[7]

As sons and daughters of the Kingdom we must discern the humanistic deception in how truth is transferred. Humanism says, 'You are of age, now you must discover your own truth and establish your own way.' In contrast, the ancient path of the Kingdom of God says, 'Truth is passed generationally, so now that you are of age you must continue in the way of the ancient path.' In the Kingdom of God the truth of the fathers is also the way of the sons, for there is only one way.

Inherent in humanistic reasoning is the suggestion that our fathers' truth began with them so we have the right to establish our own love of truth and pursue our own way. But the truth of the Kingdom of God is not found in establishing our own truth. Rather, it is being a steward of our fathers' truth and becoming responsible to the generations past in order that we might equip the generations to come.[8]

Fatherhood is all about reproduction...Fatherhood in the Kingdom of God is a description, not a position...I am a father in the Kingdom only to the degree that my spiritual genes have been reproduced in those God has brought into my life. If the reasoning, gifting and burdens that the sovereignty of God has birthed in me are not birthed in them as well, I am not their spiritual father. I may be someone they deeply respect or deeply admire, but I am not their father. I may be their guardian or even their teacher, but not their father. If the spiritual genes Father has placed in me are duplicated in them, only then am I their father.[9]

With the quotes above I hoped to establish in our minds the biblical principle of the "father-to-son" (parent-to-child) principle of generational transfer. This is the primary biblical pattern of discipleship transfer. Extended family members (grandparents, aunts and uncles, etc.) have a role to play, however, it is secondary (or complimentary) to the responsibility parents have. While this may seem obvious, it needs to be said since maturing multigenerational families will be tempted to put too much emphasis on "the clan" – what I call the horizontal family. They run the risk of forgetting that multigenerational faithfulness runs primarily through nuclear families over time – what I call, the vertical family.

With this fathering principle laid as a foundation it is safer to affirm the role of the second (subsequent) generation in contributing to the multigenerational mission. Even after all those quotes from Willis above, note what he says here:

A family mission statement should be timeless, yet relevant. It should define both the direction and the means. Every member of the family should participate in a council so there is total ownership of the family plan. Like the putting together of a puzzle, each family member will bring a piece of the overall look. When the whole family contributes, it is much easier to detect what God has ordained from the foundation of time (Ephesians 2:10). A family mission statement is something specially uncovered by the entire family. Therefore, it can be owned by the entire family. With family ownership, it will serve as a roadmap to guide a means to refocus in the midst of life's storms. A family mission statement cannot simply be presented and then expected to be enthusiastically embraced. Fathers must lead the family into a council of participation and mutual discovery.[10]

My studies and reflection on these questions have led me to suggest the following as a place to begin your thinking and planning. Assuming you are a nuclear family with minor children, fathers, with the assistance of their helpmate, should work on drafting a multigenerational family mission statement. Assume that the heart of that mission is to be adopted by your sons[11] for their own nuclear families and their descendants. While the mission is multigenerational in nature, the actions of that mission can be applied to a father's nuclear family. As mentioned earlier, a multigenerational family, while real, is something that exists throughout time; it has a certain level of abstraction. Only nuclear, extended families, and perhaps clans, in a living generation can actually steward and operate a multigenerational mission.

The primary focus of multigenerational faithfulness is the *vertical* family (father to sons in nuclear families) as opposed to the *horizontal* family (extended families and clans). Recall Pryor's statement that only some children may adopt their parents' commission. Adult sons have jurisdictional authority over their nuclear families. I recommend adult sons renew the mission of their father's convictions in a fresh way for their nuclear family and their descendants. They can discern what is abiding in their father's vision and retain those elements in their covenantal renewal while adding and modifying new convictions they receive from their heavenly Father.

The second generation of the extended family, including adult sons along with their father and mother, can create an extended family mission that is related but also distinct from the missions of each nuclear family that make up the extended family. The principle of creative ownership ("buy in") of the second generation can be preserved in two directions. The first is in renewing the multigenerational family covenant in a unique way for their own nuclear family. The second is in establishing a horizontal mission with their siblings and father at the extended family level (or clan). This complex relationship among nuclear families and their extended family will be elaborated in more detail in the chapter on governance.

My recommendation above assumes a young family is beginning this process. What if a second-generation group of adult siblings find themselves desiring to establish an extended family mission or constitution without the father's input (for whatever reason)? Or, what if you're a first generation grandfather catching this vision for the first time?

For the first scenario (adult siblings, no father) it is my recommendation that those siblings first establish a family mission statement (or strategic plan) for their own nuclear family and future descendants (vertical, multigenerational family), and only afterwards create an extended family mission or constitution for their current, living extended family (horizontal level). Why? Because of the inherent nature of generational transfer flowing primarily from father to son (child) as we saw above.

As for the second scenario (first generation grandfather catching this vision), I would encourage you to be bolder than you think you have warrant. Because you have more warrant than you probably realize. The nature of covenant means God recognizes covenantal relationships even if we don't. A grandfather is the representative head responsible for his extended family. Your adult sons are jurisdictionally heads of their own households and you must deal with them as adult children now. You cannot demand from them. However, they are not the representatives of the *extended* family – you are! They are covenantally dependent upon your blessing – a blessing with real, eternal substance (see Genesis 48 – Jacob and Joseph and his sons). You have the right to ask them to receive a multigenerational mission and vision from your fatherly authority. You can invite them to contribute to discerning and determining the family vision and mission, but ultimately, it should come primarily from you. Remember, the pattern of generational transfer is from father to son(s).

Common vs. Unique Elements of a Christian Family Mission

We are now ready to address the question of whether Christian families should have a mission that is common to all families or whether each family has a unique mission. I already revealed that the answer is yes to both. We'll look to see how that is the case starting with the common mission.

If we start by asking the question of what is the mission of a Christian as an individual, or the Church generally, most of us (hopefully!) would have the Great Commission of Jesus recorded in Matthew 28 come to mind. And we would be correct (partially, at least). It stands to reason that the same mission that is meant for Christians individually and the Church at large should be the same mission of the family. And this is true. The commissioning of our Lord to disciple the nations belongs to every Christian family. How that mission expresses itself through a multigenerational family will have distinct features compared with how it is expressed through an individual Christian or the Church at large, but it is the same mission underneath.

When it comes to the question of the Christian mission, while the Great Commission is what typically might come to mind for most Christian families, I am going to argue that the Dominion Mandate recorded in Genesis 1:26-28 (and repeated throughout Scripture) ought to be the fountainhead of Christian mission. I already alluded to this in Chapter 1 and it is now time to make the connection between the Dominion Mandate and the Great Commission.

The mandate given to Adam to bring dominion to the earth, contrary to what some Christians might assume, did not get repealed with the Fall nor the New Covenant. One way of explaining this covenantal task is to say dominion is about bringing order out of chaos. Adam was to go into the wilderness of the earth (chaos) and form it into a garden on the pattern of Eden (order and beauty). With the Fall, we learned that sin brought further disorder into the whole creation. The earth was cursed, human relationships were cursed, and the relationship between God and man was cursed. The curses upon the earth and human relationships were a direct result of the break in relationship between God and man.

We get a glimmer of hope revealed in Genesis 3:15 that one would come who would crush the head of the serpent, Satan, and thereby reverse the curse. In the call of Abraham we see this commitment from God move forward. With the promise to David that a Messianic Servant would come from his house, we get even further details of how God is going to address the problem of the curse and restore the dominion task given to man. And then the Father's only begotten Son, the Lord Jesus Christ, as determined in their eternal covenant, is sent to earth, preaching the gospel of the kingdom.

"King-*dom*" is the *dom*inion (rule) of the King. The covenantal nature of God's rule of earth is clearly that He does so through His elected representative, Man. This is why Gentry and Wellum argue that the message of the entire Bible can be summarized by the phrase, "kingdom through covenant."[12]

The heart of man was separated from God in the Fall. Man cannot be restored to his dominion task of bringing order to the chaos of the world when his own heart is in a state of "disorder." This is why the gospel of the kingdom starts with making disciples of Jesus. Men's hearts need to be reconciled with God first and from that position they can now return to the task of bringing dominion to the earth. The Great Commission flows out of the Dominion Mandate. There is an essential unity to the mission of Christians and Christian families.

Norm Willis writes,
Matthew 28:19-20 is the New Testament reiteration of the Dominion Mandate recorded in Genesis 1:28. Like divine bookends, these two mandates frame God's desire. The Dominion Mandate of Genesis 1 defines God's intent; the Great Commission of Matthew 28 defines His method.[13]

In the first chapter I referenced four "fountainheads" of the mission that is common to all families – the Dominion Mandate, the Abrahamic Covenant, the Kingdom of God, and the Great Commission of discipleship. While each has distinct emphases, I hope by now you can see their essential unity.

Now that I have argued for a common mission that Christian families should adopt, does this mean your work is done? No. Each family is responsible for interpreting this mission and articulating it in a unique way for their family. Does the mission of discipleship mean your family goes knocking on doors with evangelistic tracks every day? Does dominion mean your family is going to focus on cultural tasks outside the family or focus on the cultural development of children first? Obviously, this is a false dichotomy, but I mention it to show that your family is going to have to decide how the mission is going to be expressed. And remember, you're asking how the mission is to be done through your family, not merely through you as an individual.

Now that we have addressed the question of a mission that should be held in common among Christian families, we ask the question again – do families have unique aspects to their mission? I think the Bible gives evidence that this is so. Notice what Jeremy Pryor writes on this subject:

> Once we have a clear understanding of our mission as families we also need to consider how God may give a unique vision specifically to our family and our family line. In the Old Testament we have many examples of families who have unique callings that get passed down from generation to generation. Aaron's family was set aside to do the priestly ministry, David's family was set apart to rule, and the Korahites were gatekeepers (1 Chronicles 9:19), singers (2 Chronicles 20:19) and poets for hundreds of years who penned at least eleven of the Psalms.[14]

Norm Willis says it this way:
> Not only does every individual have a God-given purpose, but also each family has a unique purpose before God. Even as each individual in that family carries a unique God-given design, when those uniquenesses are put together in a family unit, it results in a unique family purpose. Parents must pray and discern to determine what that purpose is.[15]

I am reminded of the story of Jonadab and the Rechabites from the book of Jeremiah. As you will recall from the comments to that story in Chapter 1, Jonadab ordered his descendants to abstain from wine and they obeyed that command for at least 250 years! Remember that God affirmed that this was a good thing and blessed their multigenerational family for it. Obviously, the commission to not drink wine is not a mission that is applicable to all families of God. But apparently, it was a unique element within this family's mission.

I am also reminded of Jacob blessing his twelve sons and giving them specific multigenerational blessings that were unique to each family. And I have to consider if the

Benjamites started wondering if God had a purpose in why they were all left-handed. Throughout history we can find multiple examples of multigenerational families carrying on a common occupational pursuit.

As the founding generation, you may not perceive what the unique elements of your family mission are. Pay attention over the years and by the grace of God you may begin discerning what those unique elements are. And don't forget that this may not mature in the consciousness of the family until subsequent generations. That is okay. God is in control of this process. Which leads us to our next question.

Is The Family Mission Discovered or Determined?

Again, I already revealed the "secret" to this question that the short answer is both/and. Much of what we discussed above has at least indirectly already answered this question. If one side of the equation should predominate, I would say it is the "discovered" side. Quoting Norm Willis again, he writes:

> Family planning, from a spiritual perspective, is a matter of discernment not initiation. Proper family planning is not dreaming up something by yourself, but rather discerning the plan God has already devised.[16]

Starting with the issue of the common mission of dominion (or discipleship; there are several ways we can summarize this), this is obviously something that is discovered. It is determined by God, not a family. A family discovers this mission in Scripture. However, just as we mentioned above, every individual family does have to determine how this is to be interpreted and expressed for themselves. In that sense it is determined. And consider the possibility that your understanding of mission in Scripture may likely change (hopefully in a maturing direction) over time. When that is the case, I would expect you would need to modify your family's expression of its mission. I know this has occurred for me and our family more than once. When we change how we understand our family mission and subsequently change our articulation of it, in that sense we are determining our mission (qualified by the recognition that it is rooted in discovery).

The same holds for your family's unique aspects of its mission. Even if you notice a strong, particular passion that properly belongs to the family mission, theologically we know that God is the giver of such passions. Or, we might discover that we made a mistake in discernment. What we thought was a passion that was appropriate for the family mission, we may later determine we were foolish or naïve in assuming so. However, we can't wait forever until we have "perfect" discernment, which is unattainable. We have to act in the present at whatever level of maturity we find ourselves. So, again, in this sense we are determining our family's unique aspects of our family mission and look to God for the grace that we will mature in discernment over time.

Process versus Purpose

What do I mean by process versus purpose? I have to bring up this distinction because I was almost derailed from considering the legitimacy of crafting a family mission statement after reading material by Christian author, Michael Bunker. Bunker was critiquing the "purpose-driven" philosophy espoused by a handful of famous Christian leaders, particularly Rick Warren and Joel Osteen. Bunker was arguing that Scripture does not ask believers to determine their "purpose for life" in the way that these other Christian teachers were advocating. For example, does a local church in L.A. really know if it is supposed to "take the city for Christ"? Not surprisingly, none of these purpose-driven advocates found that a particular purpose (in God's secret, providential will) of an individual might be to die prematurely for the cause of Christ! And yet, the Bible and history have proven that many Christians have served the cause of Christ precisely through their martyrdom!

Instead, Bunker argued that Scripture asks believers to lead a "process-driven life." All believers are called to live lives of daily, common obedience. This is what we are to focus on. Most of the specific purposes God has for individuals or groups are kept in His secret will. As I reflected on this, I came to the conviction that Bunker was onto something. I despaired at the thought of losing my convictions about family mission statements.

A few days of reflection relieved my fears. Like many realities in life, there is a paradoxical relationship between this question of purpose and process. What Bunker was pointing to was real. There are many "purposes" that we dream up that probably have nothing to do with God's intent. And most of God's specific providential actions in history remain hidden from us. However, this reality does not obliterate all senses of purposeful mission in a Christian's life. There are righteous and legitimate pursuits of mission. For starters, I contemplated again the dominion mandate and great commission and determined, while they have a "process" perspective, they still more properly belong to the domain of purpose and mission. I also came to the realization that if one lives "process-driven" as Bunker was advocating, it is still the case that one *purposes* to do so. In other words, even process has a purpose perspective.

At the end of the day, what this experience taught me is that we do need to be careful in determining our family mission statements. We don't want to be creating false missions or elevating a perceived unique mission over and above the process-oriented life of common obedience.

This experience did prompt our family to make an addition to our family mission statement. It happened to coincide with our discovery of the covenantal nature of families. We added a missional component centered around the idea of covenantal faithfulness.

The principle of process over purpose does point to the need for our multigenerational family missions to have an enduring quality to them. Typically, missions are things that have an end goal date. Multigenerational missions, by their nature, are probably better if they tend toward an eschatological direction. A multigenerational mission, however, can be broken down into specific objectives that have end goal dates within a single generation. We will talk about this in the final section of this chapter. But first, let us look at some sample family mission statements that I believe will help generate ideas of your own.

Drafting Your Family Mission Statement

Before we get into how to approach drafting your family mission statement, it would be good to revisit some defining summaries of what such a statement is. Recall from above that a mission is a statement of purpose and action, applicable now as well as in the future. It is the means of successfully achieving the vision. Here is how Norm Willis defines a family mission statement:

> A family mission statement simply describes (at that particular season) the vision God has given you as a family and how you plan to get there. This family mission statement should address:
>
> - The specific plan for that particular family
> - How that plan is to be accomplished.
>
> ... Simply put, a family mission statement delineates the goals we have as a family and the way in which we plan

to get there. A family mission statement answers three primary questions:

1. Who God has defined your family to be?
2. What He has determined your family to do?
3. How He expects your family to do it?[17]

It is now time to walk through the steps to begin drafting your family mission statement.

We mentioned above that every family already has a family mission on at least a subconscious level. The first step in drafting your mission statement, then, is to discover what your subconscious family mission already is. This is a work of introspection. Start by scheduling several family meetings (i.e., with your spouse). Discuss with each other the following questions:

- What does our family spend the most amount of time on?
- What does our weekly schedule tell us about our highest values?
- What about our annual schedule?
- What do we spend most of our discretionary money on?
- What excites us the most as a family?
- When we plan future events, what subject occupies the largest amount of time we spend on planning?
- With the above questions, when you have multiple answers, organize them in a hierarchy of importance to your family.

You can add additional questions as necessary, but you can see the point is to flush out what are your family's beliefs, values, and vision by observing your family behavior. Once you have thoroughly discussed these questions (and allow this to take its time; several weeks of discussion perhaps), it is time to "reverse-engineer" your family mission. What does your family behavior tell you about what your mission is? It is imperative that you are honest with yourself, because if you have not been living intentionally, the answer will probably not be as flattering as you hope.

You may find that your family mission has a lot more to do with sports, for example, than you realized. An honest evaluation of your family may reveal a mission of something like "enjoyment of family" as a mission (did your discussions reveal that you spend more time planning family vacations than planning discipleship?). While enjoying family may be something that is good in itself, you have to ask if that is a worthy multigenerational mission.

Once you reverse-engineer your family mission by taking an honest look at your behavior, ask yourselves if this is what you want your family mission to be. Your family mission may have several components. Perhaps some of them you agree are worthy values, while others are not so worthy. If there are elements that you find are not worthy to be included in your family mission, you have some decisions to make that will radically effect the way you live.

The other part of discovery is to determine what the Word of God says about a family's mission. And guess what? It has a lot to say about what a family's mission ought to be. The previous chapters of this book already made an argument of what I think Scripture reveals on this subject (dominion, covenant, Kingdom of God, discipleship). However, you will need to take ownership of this for your family. Study this subject for yourself and come to your own conclusions (Acts 17:11). It is okay to lean on the opinions of others initially, but over time parents (and fathers particularly) should understand what Scripture teaches about the family organically, from the ground up.

From your introspective analysis and study of Scripture, there are two possibilities of pre-existing mission assumptions you've had for your family. One possibility is that some of your mission assumptions are fleshly or shallow and need to be discarded. The other possibility is that you have identified a passion area that God Himself may have put into your heart. Obviously, the first is to be rejected while the latter is to be embraced.

Once you have gone through this period of introspection, it is time to sit down and begin articulating what you think your family mission should be. As mentioned earlier, you may decide to begin writing down your family's values or vision first, and that is okay. Don't over-worry about getting your statement(s) "perfect." Your first draft is just that. Allow yourself the grace to see your family mission statement slowly mature. In time, it will "settle down."

A quick word about "word-smithing" your family mission statement. Work towards making it as concise as possible and memorable. You can (should) provide longer explanations of what the mission statements mean and imply separately — either in a constitution document or in an addendum (see comments on a Family Documents Portfolio from Chapter 2). Making your statement concise and memorable serves as a training tool for your family. You want your children to be able to repeat the statements. Your training over time will fill in the content of what those concise statements imply.

Another issue that comes up is the question of whether the family mission just includes the specific mission-component, or does it also include beliefs, values, and vision? Yes and no. They are distinct, but as mentioned earlier, mission assumes beliefs, values, and vision even if those are not articulated. For our family, while our mission statement is articulated separately from our beliefs, values, and vision, when we speak of "our family mission," conceptually we know we are also including our beliefs, values, and vision. It is shorthand for referencing the whole package. In addition, recalling our discussion of the family culture, we also assume the entirety of our family culture as being wrapped up in our family mission. The mission is our family culture applied consciously to generational transfer.

The next section provides quotes of sample family mission statements. This should help your family see how the principles outlined above are fleshed out in specific families. It will help you see both the unity and diversity in Christian family mission statements. I pray these examples will help with your family's brainstorming process in crafting your own, unique statements.

Sample Family Mission Statements[18]

Sample 1
We are a family of sons and daughters of Jesus Christ, demonstrating a Kingdom culture by training the generations to carry the vision of Christ centeredness and covenantal living through a heart of submission, with faith, passion, love and obedience, for the glory of God and the reformation of the Church.

Sample 2
The mission of our family is to create a nurturing place of faith, order, truth, love, happiness and relaxation and to provide opportunity for each individual to become responsibly independent and effectively interdependent in order to serve worthy purposes in society through understanding and living the gospel of Jesus Christ.

Sample 3
- *Make disciples*
- *Grow bodies*
- *Release the fivefold* [see Ephesians 4:11]

Sample 4
[Our] family exists to bring joy and delight to the heart of God and to take delight in Him.

Sample 5
To intentionally and purposefully minister to, fellowship with, and train God's families that are interested in kingdom expansion through fulfilling the Great Commission.

The father behind the fourth sample statement above is a friend of mine, with whom I had the pleasure to discuss the creation of his family mission statement. His experience confirmed my suspicions that all families who begin the process of creating their mission statements (or governance plan) will experience similar things – the distinctions we discussed above – common vs. unique elements, different "levels" of specificity, etc.

Talking with him about his family mission statement directed my attention to another important observation. You can see in the brief statement of his above, reference to the word, *delight*. An outsider reading this statement will not be impacted by that simple word. However, since I had the opportunity to read the much longer document my friend produced that fleshed out the explanation and implications of the mission, I learned that behind that simple word was a complex and deep theological understanding. A mere word was a label for a large world of meaning. Mission statements can appear as simplistic clichés to outsiders, but are monuments to the insiders who may have spent months or years creating them.

In our family's multi-part mission statement, the Kingdom of God is repeatedly referenced. In the concise expression of the mission statement, the idea of the Kingdom of God is not expounded. It is expounded, however, in other family documents. As my family is discipled in our understanding of the Kingdom of God, the phrase will begin to represent a "book's-worth" of ideas – something an outsider could not appreciate.

The other main thing my friend experienced in creating his family mission statement is that it "forced" him to break it down into increasingly specific components. Again, I assume most families will experience this phenomenon as they work on their mission. To this subject we turn next as we draw this chapter to a close.

Objectives, Strategy, Tactics, and Family Aspirations

Before we leave the subject of mission, we need to address some "peripheral" components that are usually discussed along with mission. While things like beliefs and vision precede mission, other concepts follow mission. Mission needs to be broken down into smaller chunks to be effective. A 100-year plan by itself, for example, doesn't answer the question of how we live out that plan this month! And one objective may have several possible ways of being accomplished – which of those ways is going to be implemented? This is the domain of strategic planning, and while there are various naming schemes, the typical headings include objectives, strategy and tactics. Consider the following distinctions between these elements:

> *Strategic Plan*: Strategy, narrowly defined, means "the art of the general" — a combination of the ends (goals) for which the group is striving and the means (policies) by which it is seeking to get there. A strategy is sometimes called a roadmap–which is the path chosen to plow towards the end vision. The most important part of implementing the strategy is ensuring the organization is going in the right direction which is towards the end vision.

Goals (aka, objectives, initiatives): When drafting a strategic plan it is necessary to develop it in a way that is easily translatable into action plans. Most strategic plans address high-level initiatives and overarching goals, but don't get translated into day-to-day projects and tasks that will be required to achieve the plan.

Tactics vs. Strategy: Strategy has to do with large-scale questions, while tactics deal with the smaller-scale, how-to questions.[19]

From time to time, and as is necessary, you will need to determine and write down more narrowly defined objectives and tactics for how your family is going to pursue its mission. I already mentioned this above, but for our family, we chose to name these *family initiatives*. In a separate document we have outlined almost a dozen specific objectives with end goal dates ranging from three to thirty years. Each initiative is tied in some way to an element of our mission statement.

Reputation Aspirations

I want to share one final category for consideration. This is a category we developed on our own. I call it Reputation Aspirations.

Reputation aspirations are just what the phrase sounds like. They may be similar to vision statements, or goals and objectives, but they are put in this terminology to help family members think about the kinds of things every family member should be known for. Not every one of them is necessarily an extremely "high" value goal and, therefore, are better in an aspiration list rather than a vision or goal list. To avoid redundancy, aspirations spelled out in the family mission and vision are not repeated in this list, however, it can be assumed those things are still aspirations.

Also, I did not intend to repeat a list of core biblical virtues with this tool (e.g., faithful, wise, etc.). This is more akin to a unique set of "second-tier" virtues. "First-tier" virtues should be assumed. It may take more than a generation or two to achieve these reputation aspirations, but codifying them will provide a standard for future family members to create training rhythms that reliably produce these characteristics.

A few examples may suffice (we'll us the fictitious "Anderson family" for illustration):
- Anderson children grow up quickly.
- Andersons embody the proverb, "jack of all trades and a master of one."
- Andersons are wise risk takers.
- Andersons are civilization builders
- Andersons are aware of the most influential cultural forces in their generation.

Chapter 4

THE FAMILY "ASSETS AND BALANCE SHEET"

The title of this chapter gives the appearance that we are going to discuss economics. However, "assets and balance sheet" are in quotation marks for a reason – while they include the traditional understanding of assets as material wealth, they are also a metaphor for the non-material wealth of a family. In actuality, the terminology of wealth is not even a metaphor for what might be called "spiritual" values, but rather, spiritual (non-material) realities are just another form of wealth.

> Consider 1 Timothy 6:18 and Matthew 6:20:
> "...be *rich* in good deeds."
> "...but lay up for yourselves *treasures* in heaven, ..."

Dozens of other Scriptures could be recalled that use some variation of traditionally economic terms of wealth to apply to non-material realities.

All the authors writing on multigenerational families uniformly speak of the idea of building and preserving a family's "assets" as a necessary perspective in successfully transmitting and protecting the family culture for generations. Different metaphors are used – wealth, assets, capital – but they all amount to the same idea.

It is necessary to draw out this "balance sheet" perspective of a multigenerational family now, as it will be used as a conceptual framework for the rest of the book. We will look at a few authors' categorization schemes to help us understand what is meant by a family's assets.

James Hughes Jr. says:
A family's wealth consists primarily of its human capital (defined as all the individuals who make up the family) and its intellectual capital (defined as everything that each individual family member knows), and secondarily of its financial capital.[1]

... Very few families have understood that their wealth consists of three forms of capital: human, intellectual, and financial. Even fewer families have understood that without active stewardship of their human and intellectual capital they cannot preserve their financial capital. In my opinion, the issue most critical to the failure of a family to preserve its wealth is concentration on the family's financial capital to the exclusion of its human and intellectual capital. A family's failure to understand what its wealth is and to manage that wealth successfully dooms that family to fulfill the shirtsleeves proverb. In fact, this concentration on financial capital may even cause it to go out of business in just one generation.[2]

Hughes asks families to think of their family wealth in terms of a balance sheet (this terminology is metaphorical). Like a multigenerational business, multigenerational families have assets and liabilities. They need to know how the family "enterprise" is doing and therefore need to measure the family's condition and progress. A family balance sheet measures its human and intellectual capital (as well as it financial) and is an attempt to measure how well a family is managing it human capital.

The following chart is adapted from James Hughes Jr.'s book, *Family Wealth*:[3]

THE FAMILY BALANCE SHEET

ASSETS
The family's total human capital including:
- Each family member's intellectual capital
- Each family member's financial capital
- Each family member's social capital

LIABILITIES
Long-term family risks:
- Failure of family governance
- Failure to understand that success requires a one-hundred-year plan
- Failure to comprehend and manage all forms of family capital, human and intellectual as well as financial

Intermediate family risks (internal):
- Death
- Divorce
- Addiction and other "secrets"
- Malthus' Law (the geometric increase of family members in each generation)
- Creditors
- Poor beneficiary/trustee relationships
- Investment programs of less than fifty years

Intermediate family risks (external):
- Inflation
- Inadequate trustee management
- Estate and other forms of transfer and wealth taxes

- Holocaust
- Acts of God
- Changes of political system
- Lack of personal security

Short-term family risks:
- Income taxes
- Market fluctuation
- No mission statement
- Lack of financial education

SHAREHOLDER EQUITY
- Are individual family members successfully pursuing happiness?
- Are the family's human capital and intellectual capital increasing when measured against the family's liabilities?
- Is the family as a whole dynamically preserving itself?
- Is the family's governance system producing more good decisions than bad by taking a seventh-generational view?

Study this chart and notice the non-material assets and liabilities. Does your family have something like a 100-year plan? If not, and if Hughes is right (remember, he is an experienced world authority on the subject), this is a liability to your multigenerational family. And my guess is that "poor trustee/beneficiary relationships" is not on most families' radar as a liability to their ability to persevere over the generations. These are some clues that today's families will need to begin adopting new paradigms if they are to transition to legacy families.

Hughes also suggests families adopt a tool that is analogous to an income statement. This tool would measure individual family members' increase or decrease in the three capitals. He mentions a "best practice" to do this is for family leaders to collect and evaluate updated resumes and personal mission statements on an annual basis.[4]

Lee Brower wrote a book titled, *The Brower Quadrant*. The following is how he categorized a family's wealth:[5]

Core Assets:
- Family
- Health
- Happiness and well-being
- Values, etc.

Contribution Assets:
- Charitable contributions
- Taxes vs. choice and control, etc.

Experiential Assets:
- Education
- Experiences (good and bad)
- Reputation
- Traditions, etc.

Financial Assets:
- Money
- Real Estate
- Retirement plans
- Businesses
- Jewelry, etc.

And finally, the following is how Hausner and Freeman categorize family wealth:[6]

Human Capital:
- Effective parenting and grand parenting
- Communication
- Consensus building

- Team building
- Conflict resolution
- Leadership training
- Values, morals, ethics
- Spirituality, and
- Goal setting.

Intellectual Capital:
- Education
- Career choices
- Coaching and mentoring
- Governance
- Rights and roles of trustees and beneficiaries.

Financial Capital:
- Creating wealth
- Managing/investing wealth
- Effective transfer strategies
- Financial parenting (preparing the next generation to be responsible stewards of wealth)
- Family business issues, and
- Understanding the psychology of money.

Social Capital:
- All the philanthropic activities of the family, from check writing to family foundations and donor-advised funds, and volunteer time to full-time public service.

With the above examples you can again see the unity and diversity in how a family thinks of its wealth. You will have to determine for your own family how you want to categorize and label your family assets (and liabilities).

The authors above have two messages they each emphasize in their own way regarding a family's assets ("balance

The Family "Assets and Balance Sheet"

sheet"). First, families must increase each aspect of their wealth categories to preserve their wealth over time. Because liabilities always exist, mere preservation without growth will necessarily lead to dissipation and death of family wealth.

Second, and more importantly, they emphasize that it is the growth of the non-material assets that ultimately will preserve the financial assets of a family. And a corollary to this is that the purpose of a family's financial assets is to grow and preserve a family's human (core) assets.

> Here is how Hughes says it:
> To be sure, not every thriving member of a family will directly increase the family's financial capital. Individually, however, achieving one's highest intellectual and emotional capacity should enhance the family's overall capital in ways that will increase the family's financial capital, if in no other way than by making each person the best family shareholder, beneficiary, or representative he can be.
>
> With growth of human and intellectual capital comes a high probability of growth of financial capital. Without growth of human and intellectual capital, financial capital may still grow, but it will not matter to the family's ability to preserve its wealth over the long term, since the family will go out of business as its human assets become less and less valuable.
>
> Where, then, does financial capital fit in, if it alone cannot assure long-term wealth preservation? A family's financial capital can provide a powerful tool with which to promote the growth of its human and intellectual capitals. ... Without intellectual capital, undereducated family members with all the money in the world will not make enough good decisions. Successful long-term wealth preservation lies in understanding that it is the growth of a family's

human and intellectual capital that determines its success, and that the growth of its financial capital provides a major tool for achieving this success.[7]

These are secular authors. Where they speak of "human" assets/wealth, I would qualify this by saying that a Christian family's financial assets are to be used only indirectly for their "human" assets, pointing beyond themselves to their mission, which is God and Kingdom-centered.

Chapter 5

FAMILY GOVERNANCE AND SUCCESSION

In Chapter 2 we introduced James Hughes Jr.'s insight into the necessity *and centrality* of practicing governance to successfully preserve family wealth (material and spiritual) over the generations. As we review Hughes' theory on the place of family governance below, we remember he is a secular author. We can make the necessary discernment to purge the secular elements while preserving the useful insights. Here is Hughes' philosophy summarized:

    I. **The Question**: Can a family successfully preserve its wealth for more than one hundred years or for at least four generations?

   II. **The Problem**: The history of long-term wealth preservation in families is a catalog of failures epitomized by the proverb, "shirtsleeves to shirtsleeves in three generations."

  III. **The Theory**:
      a. Preservation of long-term family wealth is a question of human behavior.
      b. Wealth preservation is a dynamic process of group activity, or governance, that must be successfully

re-energized in each successive generation to overcome the threat of entropy.
c. The assets of a family are its individual members.
d. The wealth of the family consists of the human and intellectual capital of its members. A family's financial capital is a tool to support the growth of the family's human and intellectual capital.
e. To successfully preserve its wealth, a family must form a social compact among its members reflecting its shared values, and each successive generation must reaffirm and readopt that social compact.
f. To successfully preserve its wealth, a family must agree to create a system of representative governance through which it actively practices its values. Each successive generation must reaffirm its participation in that system of governance.
g. The mission of family governance must be the enhancement of the pursuit of happiness of each individual member. This will enhance the family as a whole and further the long-term preservation of the family's wealth: its human, intellectual, and financial capital.

IV. **The Solution**: A family can successfully preserve wealth for more than one hundred years if the system of representative governance it creates and practices is founded on a set of shared values that express that family's "differentness."

V. **The Practice**: Families should employ multiple quantitative and, more importantly, qualitative techniques to enable them, over a long period of time, to make slightly more positive than negative decisions regarding the employment of their human, intellectual, and financial capital.[1]

There are some key elements that I want to emphasize from Hughes' summary. The first is to take note of the identification of governance as group decision making. Following this is the expectation that the family makes slightly better decisions as a group over time. Finally, it's important to note the point that every subsequent generation must reaffirm and readopt the "social compact" (I would say this is the family covenant for Christian families; in other words, families are to practice *covenant renewal*).

As we examine below the different considerations that go into the governance system that a family creates, keep in mind that your conclusions will be incorporated into a family constitution. Much of what is covered here is a reflection of my own decisions. I am not assuming your family is to "copy" these decisions, but rather I intend to provide you with the structure and considerations for making your own family constitution. At the same time, I will be honest with what I have found to be a "best practice."

Succession and Membership

We will start with the question of succession. What exactly is being passed down? Every parent's influence – good or bad – will be passed down to at least their immediate heirs no matter what they do. But a purely passive approach guarantees that a specific, covenantal intention will *not* be guarded over multiple generations. Multigenerational families cannot afford to rely on passive influence.

In traditional estate planning, what is formally passed down is, well, an estate! Money. Property. In a Christian multigenerational family, what is primarily passed on to the next generation is a *covenantal stewardship*.

The covenant with Abraham is the paradigm that Christian families still follow. While the covenant was given first to Abraham, recall that God also made covenant with his faithful descendants *at the same time.* Abraham was the first steward. He was to disciple his son to receive this covenantal stewardship from him (succession) in a manner that it would get passed from generation to generation.

Anyone considering succession unavoidably realizes that not all children remain faithful and therefore can become unworthy stewards. This brings up the question of membership. As a Christian-covenantal-multigenerational family, biological descent is an insufficient criteria for membership. Consider how Sutton addresses this issue:

> Of course, to apply this concept of [covenant] marriage and family, one must love the covenant more than he loves his children. Family continuity should be built on the covenant. Children should be taught to see the connection between covenant faithfulness and inheritance, both spiritual and material. Christians are not to subsidize evil, which is what unconditional inheritance does in a world of sin and covenant-breaking.[2]

We will deal with the question of membership for the governing bodies of a family below. The question here is who should be a member of the multigenerational family. It simply does not make sense for an adult family member who denies Christ to be considered part of a specifically covenantal-multigenerational Christian family. How can such an individual confess allegiance to a family covenant that expressly honors the Lordship of Christ? It is a flat contradiction and impossibility.

You may respond by saying that such a family member is still "part of the family," and you would be right, but only right in a sense. Earlier, I outlined the different "levels" of a family. To those distinctions, we now have to add another. I'll call it the *natural* family. At first I wanted to use the term, *the biological family*, however, that does not allow for adopted members. We'll define the natural family as the civil-legal family, which would include children born of natural descent as well as adopted children.

Now that we have this additional category, we know how to think of adult children who do not profess faith in Christ. They remain members of the natural family, however, they cannot remain members of the multigenerational *covenantal* family. It should not be assumed this scenario automatically implies some kind of strained relationship with unbelieving family members, nor does it imply there is no covenantal relationship whatsoever. They are loved as a natural family member and 1 Timothy 5:8 (among other considerations) informs us that we still have covenantal duties to our unbelieving natural family members. As we will see below, multiple covenantal relationships among multiple parties can (and will) exist at the same time.

Making this distinction between the natural family and the covenantal family also helps with another possibility. For our multigenerational family we have added the possibility of a *"multigenerational family adoption."* We have recognized that for unique reasons, the family may determine to "adopt" an individual into the Multigenerational Family. This is not a traditional, legal adoption in conjunction with state authorities. It would most likely only be used with adults. There may be unforeseen reasons to bring into the multigenerational family an outside man who marries a covenant family daughter, for example.

Another possibility would involve a descendent of the *natural* family who is no longer a covenant family member due to his father or grandfather breaking covenantal ties. In other words, consider the fact that when a father breaks covenant with the multigenerational family, he excludes his descendants from participating in the covenantal, multigenerational family as well. What if one of those descendants learns of his ancestors' covenantal, multigenerational family and desires to rejoin that family? The Family Council may decide to accept this descendent into the Covenant Family upon meeting required qualifications.

In regards to minor children, for our family, we have deemed they are automatically members of the multigenerational family, but that they have to personally affirm the family covenant when they become adults. In practice, this means that when they become an adult they have to formally and confessionally affirm the beliefs, values, and mission of the family if they want to remain a member in the *multigenerational-covenantal* family.

This brings up the question of when children are to be considered adults. And along with that, it also introduces the question of jurisdiction that we alluded to before.

Sphere Sovereignty and Jurisdiction

The term "sphere sovereignty" was first popularized by Abraham Kuyper in the late 19th century as it primarily applied to the relationships among the family, church, and state. The idea is that each of these covenantal institutions needs to recognize their God-ordained jurisdictional boundaries. For example: the state is not to take authority in areas that God's law has reserved for the family (e.g., education); the family is not to take authority in areas reserved for the church (e.g., excommunication) or state (e.g., capital punishment).

The same sphere sovereignty principle applies to jurisdictions of other social relationships including the parent-adult child relationship. One of the defining features of "becoming an adult" is that certain responsibilities parents had for their minor children are transferred to their adult children. And with the transfer of that responsibility is also transferred jurisdictional authority. An adult son is now his own "head of household."[3] That new "household" is at what we might call the nuclear family level. A new "nuclear family" has been born in seed. Father and son relate to each other as jurisdictional "equals" as it pertains to their respective nuclear families. A father should not have formal, *jurisdictional* authority to *determine* what happens in his son's newly established nuclear household. However, he may continue to carry an authority of fatherly *influence* that a son can choose to receive or not.

In addition to the creation of a new nuclear family head, when a first son becomes an adult, a new extended family is created. There are now two generational heads that can covenantally relate to each other. I would argue that the pattern in Scripture would recognize that the father is the representative (covenantal) head of this new extended family. This does not give the father the right to intrude into the son's nuclear household jurisdiction. That would be a sphere sovereignty violation. We recognize that there are now two spheres with different law-order boundaries. Father and son(s) can choose to covenantally relate to each other as an extended family with their father recognized as an extended family head (with that headship restricted to the extended family, and not to each son's nuclear family).

Transition to Adulthood

Does the Bible recognize some kind of formal transition into adulthood? Is there some kind of covenantal break between children and their parents? Is there an age or stage? Or an event – like a coming of age ceremony, or marriage? If there is a break, is it completely discontinuous or do some covenantal child-parent bonds continue for adult children and their parents?

Cultures have practiced this in various ways throughout history. The Western version is perhaps the weakest ever practiced (if it exists at all). If the Bible does assume this in some form, it certainly is not explicit. Like many things, my guess is that the Bible gives many principles and examples upon which families are free to make wise judgments in application.

Jews have used the ages of thirteen (boys) and twelve (girls) to mark this transition with their bar-mitzvah and bat-mitzvah ceremonies. Some Christian families have looked to the example of Jesus in the synagogue at the age of twelve as a standard for this transition. The example of Israelite males being eligible for enlistment in the army at the age of twenty is another possible source.

It is probably more than coincidence that this range from twelve to twenty closely mirrors the typical period of puberty. God's design of puberty appears to be a creational indication that the transition from childhood to adulthood is a slow progression rather than a single event.

The Genesis 2:24 command that a man is to "leave" his father and mother and "cleave" to his wife seems to indicate that this is a covenantal transition.[4] Does this mean that adult children who have not yet married (or who never will marry) continue the same kind of relationship with their parents as when they were minors? Hermeneutically, we are putting too much burden on Genesis 2:24 to require it to speak to the transition into adulthood apart from the question of marriage. It speaks primarily to the creation of a new covenant family being created with a new marriage. When that occurs, a man has a new family which his primary orientation is towards.

That man still may very well transition into full adulthood before marriage. In the absence of specific Scriptural parameters for this, coupled with several indications that such a transition occurs (e.g., adult Israelite males twenty years of age being eligible for the army), it would appear this is an area where families are free to make wise judgments. I have found that when there is freedom in areas such as these, looking to a given culture's "default" customs has some merit. Why? Many of these customs are enhanced, or are only possible, when the broader culture participates in them. In the contemporary American culture, that default age is eighteen.

I would not deny a family's prerogative to declare their thirteen-year-old children ready to enter into full adulthood. The problem I have with this is that I doubt such parents would expect (or permit) their sons to be ready to fully support themselves economically or to be ready to marry. In what sense are they "full adults" if they are not ready or permitted to do this? For the status of adulthood to have substance, I think those characteristics need to be in place, at least in terms of capacity (rather than actuality).

This is an issue we are still working on for our family. On the one hand, we do not agree with the culture's prolonging adolescence and think that children should be ushered into adulthood much sooner. At the same time, this transition needs to have substance. We have entertained the idea of using the age of sixteen since this is a time in our culture that a child (young adult) can obtain a driver's license (substantive enablement for economic support) as well as be legally emancipated.

There is also the issue of "age versus stage." Should an age be used to mark this transition or should certain marks of maturity be used to recognize this transition? These are decisions your family will have to make.

Governance System Options

To repeat what was acknowledged earlier, the task of choosing a governance system for your family really is first applicable at the extended family level. The nuclear family has a governance system that is sufficiently described in the Bible. The husband is the head of the household and his wife is his helpmeet in administering the family's task of dominion.

With the extended family, the question of governance is not so clear and decisions will have to be made. What will feel strange is that parents of young families will begin drafting governance systems that will not be fully applicable until several years into the future. And depending on a family's individual convictions, adoption of those governance rules may include the need for adult children to agree to them before adoption, or even contributing to the creative process beforehand. I recommend that parents of young families work on drafting a template with the recognition that their adult children may very well contribute to the system before its formal adoption in the future.

In addition to drafting a governance system for the extended family, families can envision a future in which a clan will govern itself separately from its many extended families that make it up. While the work of creating clan governance can be put off to the future, I have found it is a strategically beneficial training opportunity for young families to begin envisioning how this will work for their multigenerational family.

James Hughes reminds his readers that there are only so many governance options families have to choose from. He says that since Aristotle first outlined them, the options include an aristocracy, an oligarchy, a republic, a democracy, and a tyranny.[5] He goes on to argue that from his experience working with families, the republic form is the best option for families for at least two reasons.[6] The first is rooted in the principle that people tend to not willingly give up some freedom without the expectation that they will be rewarded with greater freedom for doing so. The second reason comes from the observation that human beings typically do not willingly enter a group unless they believe they are free to change it or leave it.

For the reasons Hughes mentions, I agree that a republican[7] form of government is good, however, I think it is not fully applicable until the family reaches the level of a clan.[8] There are just not enough family heads in an extended family for the need of elected representatives. For extended family governance, I recommend the application of consensus decision making with chief deference given to the extended family head (founding father).

David Bork records this Wikipedia description of consensus decision making:

> Consensus decision-making is a group decision-making process that seeks the consent, not necessarily the agreement, of participants and the resolution of objections. Consensus is defined by Merriam-Webster as, first, general agreement, and second, group solidarity of belief or sentiment. It has its origin in a Latin word meaning, literally, "feel together." It is used to describe both the decision and the process of reaching a decision. Consensus decision-making is thus concerned with the process of reaching a consensus decision, and the social and political effects of using this process. Consensus should not be confused with unanimity or solidarity.[9]

Bork goes on to say:

> The underlying principle of consensus decision-making is the commitment to a process that allows for all parties to contribute ideas and to feel positive about their interaction and role in the group.
>
> ... In consensus decision-making, the objective is the "common good" of the group. The process emphasizes relationship-building, which is grounded in trust and cooperation.
>
> ... It is well known that trust is the essential element to all long term relationships. Voting puts trust at risk ...[10]

It is good to remember that a family (even at the extended level and beyond) is covenantal rather than merely political. The basis of the relationship is one of trust and love among the members. Merely political or economic relationships may have warrant to recognize a foundation of mistrust (contract vs. covenant) with a mutual beneficial goal in mind. Families do not have this "luxury."

This is not to say that an element of voting, or a recognition of hierarchical leadership, is absolutely excluded from systems rooted in consensus. In my observation of consensus-based options, there are several nuanced options available to guard against individuals blocking group action as well as options for recognizing senior authorities. Recall Bork's comment that consensus should not be confused with unanimity or solidarity. Rather, the emphasis is on including every member in the decision-making process in a meaningful way.

It is not the place here to outline the details and all the options of various governance systems. Assuming your family has decided to pursue multigenerational disciplines, one of your assignments will be to thoroughly research your governance options.

Our Family's Governance Assumptions

I have found it exceedingly difficult to summarize all the options families can consider in planning governance in some kind of "neutral" way. At the risk of unduly influencing families with our particular family's decisions, in what follows I will share some of our particular long-term governance assumptions and plans. Please read this as something of a "testimony" that may help in coming to your own conclusions. And please keep in mind that our family's understanding and decisions are always evolving.

The Firstborn

A good entry point into explaining our family governance system is to begin with typical succession or estate planning regarding the transference of material wealth. We have decided to distribute our estate on the principle of the double-portion to the firstborn.[11] We are not doing this because we think it is the only "biblical way" of practicing inheritance for all believers (i.e., carried over from old covenant to new covenant). Perhaps it is, but I have yet to be convinced. We have chosen this because it at least has biblical precedent and we are less confident in the modern Western practices.

If this is a new thought for you and your first reaction is that this is somehow "unfair," that is a good indication that you don't understand the principle of the firstborn. In fact, the opposite is more accurate. The firstborn doesn't get "double" the material goodies for his own pleasure. Rather, he gets "double" the responsibility. From a purely selfish standpoint, no one would want to hold the status of firstborn. In any group, each individual is personally responsible for their part. However, there is always someone who is also responsible for the whole group. In a business, if an employee fails at something, he is personally responsible, but his immediate supervisor is also responsible. The CEO is not going to talk directly to the employee who failed, rather, he holds the supervisor responsible.

The principle of the firstborn recognizes that while all sons have an individual responsibility to steward the family covenant, the firstborn has a higher responsibility to see that the whole family is being faithful. The "double-portion" of material assets is given precisely to match the higher responsibility. Again, it is not for the firstborn's consumption. It is a stewardship to be used on behalf of the entire family's covenantal mission.

The principle of covenantal membership discussed above applies to the status of firstborn as well. While the biological (or natural) firstborn, by default, is assigned the status of covenantal firstborn (held as a beneficiary), that status may be assigned to another son if the biological firstborn proves to be unfaithful to the family covenant. The pattern of second sons (especially Esau and Jacob) receiving the right of the firstborn in the Bible is ample evidence for the legitimacy of this practice.

I mentioned that the biological firstborn holds the status of firstborn as a beneficiary. What this means is that the full rights, privileges, and responsibilities are not transferred to the firstborn until later in life. The pattern in the Bible is for this to occur at the time of anticipating the father's death. Believing this is an area of freedom, in our family we have chosen for this transition to occur when the founding father is in his seventies. The principle behind that (from our studies of best practices in multigenerational families) is a recognition of stage-of-life characteristics. Adults in their fifty- to seventy-year-old range are in a prime condition for higher order governance. They have developed wisdom and they still have sufficient energy to actively govern the family. Seniors in their latter years, while full of wisdom, begin losing the energy required to actively govern complex family life.

On Daughters and Inheritance

Following our understanding of biblical (Old Testament) patterns, we have chosen to reserve the passing of inheritance to sons. I'll briefly address the potential objections to this conviction. If one claims this is unjust *now*, it seems to follow that it was also unjust of God to establish this system in the old covenant. "But that was the old covenant," one might say. Let's assume it was something not to be carried over to the new covenant. It would still stand that if it is unjust today, it would be unjust then. Covenant administration changes are not changes in eternal justice.

A second objection might be fueled by an assumption that a conviction like this can only be motivated by some form of fundamentalist, unenlightened, misogynistic bigotry. It's certainly possible that this is true for some families. It does not follow that this is true for all families. A family can be motivated out of a biblical conviction that this is a legitimate option for families.

The primary reason why we have chosen this option is that we do not want to undermine the role of our daughters' future husbands as providers and protectors of their wives and families. If a daughter from a wealthy family brings into a marriage a large promised inheritance from her family, it severely tests whether a husband of modest means is truly his bride's provider.

At the time of this writing, we have not sufficiently researched what a dowry system would look like in our modern culture, however, this is something we intend to explore. Needless to say, should our daughters' husbands ever abandon them, the full resources of the family are ready to supply their need.

Before we leave this subject, I want to address a possible misunerstanding. I am sensitive to the reality that there is a small constituency among believers who hold to a complimentarian theology who are indeed guilty of holding an unbiblical disrespect of women. The best response I have read regarding this subject is from Doug Wilson in his book, *Reforming Marriage*. He critiques those who hold the idea that the Bible teaches there is a general submission of all women to all men. He writes:

> "So the Bible teaches submission of one woman to one man, and not one woman to all men. A woman can cheefully and graciously acknowledge that a certain

man can be a godly Christian leader, but that he is not capable of being that for *her*. The converse of this is that godly men should cheerfully grant that the world contains many women who are, on an individual level, *his* betters." [12]

First Generation Estate and Family Council

In our current family plan, when sons reach the age of majority, they are asked to begin drafting mission statements and policy and procedures for their anticipated nuclear family. These documents should take on greater specificity at the time of the son's marriage with the goal of reaching conclusion at the birth of his first child. Family heads have the authority and need the freedom to establish their nuclear-family-specific goals and policies. Some aspects of the mission statements and other nuclear family policies may be legitimate "secrets" of a nuclear family. Heads of families will be expected to share the core of their family's mission, values, and beliefs to demonstrate their compatibility with the larger levels of the multigenerational family constitution (Extended Family Constitution).

When the firstborn reaches the age of majority and covenantally chooses to remain in the multigenerational family, the Extended Family Estate will be created.[13] Initially, this will be some kind of holding entity for the multigenerational family's assets. At first it will receive contributions from the Founder's Family Estate and the firstborn's new estate (primarily income contribution at the beginning as he will not have much in the way of assets).[14] As the founder's other sons become adult Family Covenant Members, they will begin contributing to the Extended Family Estate at that time.

What we are calling the Family Council is the body of members with the authority to amend the Extended Family

Covenant and Constitution and otherwise enforce constitution rules.

The Family Council really becomes applicable when the second generation reaches an age of maturity to contribute wise decisions to the family. At the beginning, the founding father (with his wife) alone carries the role and responsibilities of what the council will possess (there is no other possibility). Sons of the founding father who are Covenant Family Members will become Family Council Members at the age of twenty-five.[15] The requirement of the age of twenty-five reflects the need for a man to grow in experience and wisdom before contributing to weighty matters affecting a large extended family. While an older man will possess more wisdom, it is also desirous that men enter into important decision-making processes as soon as reasonably possible.

The twenty-five-year-old eligibility does not mean that younger members cannot contribute to significant family matters in family business meetings. It is just official policy that until the age of twenty-five, their contribution to matters of the Family Covenant and Constitution are at the sole discretion of the founder (or older siblings already on the Family Council).

The Family Council will meet for official business at least bi-annually, but preferably quarterly. At a minimum, standard best practices for business meetings will be observed including pre-distribution of an agenda, rules of order and record keeping of meetings.

Before the inauguration of the Clan (see below), decision-making will be on a consensus basis with chief deferment given to the Extended Family Head. This will be the Founding Father at first and then later the Firstborn of the Founding Father when he becomes the Extended Family Head. This deferment is not official, but a matter of respect and pragmatism when certain decisions are being found hard to make. If the family cannot operate on a consensus basis at this first-generation level, it is perhaps not worthy of continuing as a Multigenerational Family!

A Family Covenant Member may also need to be removed from membership if they sufficiently contradict the Family Covenant and are unwilling to leave of their own accord. For a member who persistently walks in contradiction in thought or practice to the Family Covenant, the Family Council will become responsible to remove that member. In the unfortunate event of needing to remove a family member from the Multigenerational Covenant Family, approval of the Extended Family Head and a supermajority of four-fifths of the other family council members (not including the family member under consideration of removal) is needed.

Clan Governance

As I mentioned earlier, it is up to your family whether or not you begin preparing your family to transition to a clan. For the reasons I mentioned earlier, I recommend that you do.[16] In what follows, I wanted to share with families some of our thinking of how governance intersects with mature (read, post-second-generation/clan) multigenerational families. At the risk of repeating this too often, this is a provisional template of we the founding generation's thinking. We assume our sons will creatively contribute to a final form of such a governance system if, Lord willing, there is a will to do so in the future.

When the second grandson of the Founder becomes of majority age, this is the triggering event for the inauguration of the Family Clan.[17] The reason for waiting for the second grandson to reach majority age is that this is the time (assuming they qualify as Family Covenant Members) when that generation can begin to covenant together. At this triggering event, the Firstborn of the Founder and Extended Family Head becomes the Clan Head. The Clan Head's brothers then become Extended Family Heads of their own family lines. The new Clan Head at the same time will no longer hold the privileges and authority of the Extended Family Head over his brother's descendants, though he will still have that role and authority over his own Extended Family.

As the multigenerational family grows to become a Clan, the relationships among all the various components of the family will become more complex.

When the Clan is constituted the various Extended Families will establish their own Covenants and Constitutions and the Clan will establish its own Covenant and Constitution. It is expected that the spirit and core of the original multigenerational family covenant and constitution will continue into these new/renewed family covenants, but fresh expressions are expected as well. It is expected that the Clan Constitution will take on a larger group perspective as the vast majority of the activities of fulfilling the family mission can only be carried out on the nuclear family level.

For Extended Families to remain Covenant Members of the Clan Covenant, their Extended Family Covenant may not contradict the Clan Covenant in *substantive matters* (differences in minor, peripheral points are expected). This suggests the possibility of portions of the family removing themselves from the Clan Covenant or being removed.

In addition to the creation of new Extended Families with their own Extended Family Covenants, at this time, new Extended Family Estates will be created. As far as it is reasonably possible, the original Extended Family Estate will be split up among the now multiple Extended Family Estates along the same principle of the double portion. The Clan Head's Extended Family receives the double portion. It is recognized this redistribution may be unwieldy given a variety of assets involved. An exact proportioning is not necessary. This is a guiding principle that the Family Council will use in making a decision on the redistribution of the original Extended Family Estate.

In addition to the creation of new Extended Family Estates, the creation of the Clan Estate will be established. The initial funding, allocation, and distribution of the newly established Clan Estate will be left to the Family Council.

I recognize the forgoing may appear unnecessarily complex. Trust me, these complexities are inevitable if your family is ever to evolve into a mature clan. As far as the complexity, I don't expect this will be immediately intuitive. Spend some time thinking about it and it will become clear to you soon enough.

A Confederated Republic or a Covenantal Aristocracy?

We have already reviewed the multigenerational family experts who make arguments for consensus decision-making systems on the one hand as well as a republic system on the other hand. Both have their merit and are more appropriate in certain contexts (particularly the size of the decision-making body). In some ways, a hybrid of these systems can be incorporated into family governance plans.

Until recently, we intended to *exclusively* apply the republic model of governance (patterned on the American system in particular) to our family at the clan level and beyond. We intend to retain some aspects of a republic but have come to realize that our family system will be characterized by features that are distinct from a republic. I will highlight those difference in a moment. In the meantime, let us look at those elements of a republic system that we intend to retain.

Our family intends to follow a decentralized emphasis of authority. The larger units are not authoritative over the smaller units. The Extended Family unit is not authoritative over a given Family Head and his household. The Clan is not authoritative over Extended Families. Following the principle of a confederated republic, the smaller units voluntarily release some of their authority over to the larger units. With the right of voluntary membership comes the right of voluntary secession.

At the inauguration of the Clan, the family intends to institute a system that will have features of a confederated republic. This will include a bicameral Legislative Branch, an Executive Branch, and a Judicial Branch. While this level of formal organization may not be absolutely necessary for the administration of the Clan, it will strategically lay the groundwork for operating as a Tribe in the seventh generation.

Typically, two elements are emphasized as the defining features of a republic. The first is representation and the second is law. In regards to representation, it is said that civil governors (legislators, magistrates, etc.) are elected by the (franchised) people to represent them in civil governance. In regards law, it is said that "the law" is the rule of the land rather than the will of a monarch or the will of a majority (democracy).

These characteristics are true as far as they go, however, without further clarification they can be misleading. When a republic is contrasted with a democracy, what needs to be said is that it is contrasted with a *pure* democracy (the majority vote of *all* the franchised citizens). Republics in Western systems can be a type of democracy–representative democracy. As regards a claim to be the exclusive system of law-based governance, that is a misnomer. While monarchies have certainly devolved into tyrannies where the will of the king becomes the law of the land, they can technically operate as the executives of a law that is outside of the king. Republics can, and have become, just as tyrannical as monarchies.

Notice how certain non-Western nations have the term republic as part of their name. Think of today's People's

Republic of China, or the former Union of Soviet Socialist Republics. Westerners today do not think of these nations as exemplifying what is meant by a Western republic, such as the basis on which the United States of America was founded. However, from recent studies, I have come to realize that the term, *republic*, can legitimately be applied to these otherwise tyrannous regimes.

I believe the essential element of what a republic is can be discerned from its etymological base—*res publica*—"the public thing." The "public thing" is "the people" as a public group and as opposed to the private domain of the king—his kingdom. When a republic is set in contrast primarily to a monarchical system, you can see why communist states can appropriately be described as republics—they are, after all, supposed to be a *people's* government—the domain of the public rather than a private individual or family of inheritance.

Reformational philosopher, D F M Strauss explains it this way:

> Whereas a *kingdom* belonged to a king—as his private property—the state is a *public legal institution* that is designed to serve the *public interest*. This is the authentic meaning of the Latin expression *res publica*.
>
> This public legal character of the state entails that the state is by definition a republic; a public legal institution. Therefore, strictly speaking, it is not correct to employ the term 'republic' as designating some or other *form of organization* of the state. By referring to the republican nature of the state, no specific *form of government* ought to be envisaged. In the case of monarchies (distinct from republics) Machiavelli believed that the king has the power (referred to as a *kingdom*), and in the case of the latter, where sovereignty belongs to the people, it is designated as a *republic*.[18]

This may have been a long diversion on political theory, however, it is the background to a proposal I am entertaining for our multigenerational family governing philosophy. As a provisional label, I have coined the term, *covenantal aristocracy*, to describe our family governance system. Why?

Aristocracy implies a governance system that assumes governing offices are inherited. A multigenerational family governance system must, by definition, incorporate inheritance on some level. While our Western biases balk at such an idea, this conclusion is undeniable. I think we just need to be honest with it.

Aristocracy also contrasts with mere monarchy. As mentioned above, power in the clan and beyond should be decentralized. Aristocracy shares the characteristic of inheritance with monarchy, but sees governmental authority widely distributed. It can recognize the reality that individual families are already covenantally represented by family heads that have unique jurisdiction within their own families.

Some might critique the idea of an aristocratic element by arguing that not all such inheritors are gifted for leadership roles. This critique is assuming the primary role of representative heads is *technical leadership* capacity. However, the primary stewardship of *covenantal* heads is, rather, responsibility. When they lack technical leadership qualities they are responsible to appoint technically competent people to execute necessary tasks. Moses appointed an Aaron. And as I've heard my friend, Jeremy Pryor, say more than once – it is said that "*fathers* [covenantal heads] *don't meet every need, they make sure every need is met.*"

There is Scriptural precedent that "the people" are entrusted with the responsibility of electing their leaders, however, those leaders are then accountable to govern according to the law of God, not the will of the people. Dennis Woods says it this way:

In Scripture, "the people" en masse are generally not regarded as competent to rule in civil or church government. However, they are seen as competent to identify those individuals in their midst who are competent to rule by virtue of a track record of Spirit-filled service.[19]

Adding the qualifying term, *covenantal*, to our coined label, *covenantal aristocracy*, adds the following characteristics.

First, it both resembles and contrasts with constitutional government. We know that in a constitutional monarchy, for example, the king is not above the law of the constitution but is supposed to govern in terms of it and is indeed supposed to be subject to the law himself. A covenant is constitutional in the sense of marking the law and terms of a relationship, but as discussed above, it is "more than" a constitution (or contract) in that it is a relationship oriented around familial loving trust.

Secondly, it allows a family to modify its family rules beyond limitations of generic aristocracy. For our family it means we are free to incorporate a republican, or presbyterian, element into the family governance. Once an extended family emerges into the clan stage, extended families will elect family representatives to sit on the lower branch of the Clan Congress. Larger extended families will therefore have larger proportional representation (the upper chamber will be occupied by extended family heads – the aristocratic principle).

Finally, qualifying a family governance system as *covenantal* recognizes that the Law-Word of God is the underlying law of the family rather than the mere will of the family governors.

Alliances and Treaties

As your multigenerational family grows over the decades, it will become a powerful force. Like Father Abraham's family, you will have to face the reality that your family will need to consider formal relationships with other parties (I say, "parties," because they may be individuals, families, or corporations—business, civic, or otherwise).

The nature of those agreements will vary depending on the other party and the kind of relationship involved. Dennis Woods provides an insightful distinction into this dilemma.[20] He recounts the story of Abraham and the king of Sodom in the joint effort to rescue Lot. Abraham allied himself with the (pagan) king of Sodom (the Bible actually uses the word for *ally* or *confederate*) to gain help in rescuing Lot. After the victory, the king offers a permanent alliance with Abraham but Abraham refuses. While it was compatible with Abraham's relationship with God to temporarily work with the king of Sodom, Abraham did not acknowledge a fundamental unity with the king of Sodom. He refused the king's offer and acknowledged that God was the source of the victory, not the coalition. I have come to use the following two labels for these two general formal relationship possibilities—an *Enduring Alliance* or a *Temporary Coalition*.

An enduring alliance should be reserved for those relationships that sufficiently align with your family's covenantal beliefs, values, and mission. Temporary coalitions are for relationships that serve your family's mission, but where the other party's whole culture is not sufficiently compatible with your family's mission. Temporary coalitions are more akin to treaties.

The most common opportunity for an "enduring alliance" is the marriage of a family's children—and daughters particularly. While bringing a daughter-in-law into your family should certainly constitute an alliance with another family, from the biblical perspective that is assumed here, such a wife is covenantally submitting to your son's vision and dominion responsibility. For our daughters, however, we are sending them to another family's jurisdictional sphere. This is the most important enduring alliance a father and mother can make. We ought to be preparing our daughters to be noble queens and looking for sons-in-law whose family mission complements our own. Our multigenerational covenantal missions are not about serving our own families. They are about the expansion of the Kingdom of God. Praise God when we have the opportunity to send noble queens to worthy sons-in-law who will advance the Kingdom of God!

Recognizing the inherent biblical duty to care for the material needs of relatives (1 Timothy 5:8), alliances or treaties may be appropriate to safeguard and provide for relatives who are not covenant family members.

Theory on Multiple Covenant Relationships

I draw your attention again to imagine the future – the family is in its fifth generation with multiple nuclear and extended families and a clan. I mean really imagine it – estimate how many family members, extended families and nuclear families this might entail. It is inevitable that there is going to be a great diversity and complexity in these relationships. How is the family at large, and individually (nuclear families), going to governmentally relate to each other?

As I have thought about this problem, I have come to recognize that the higher up we go on the family-level-chain, the covenantal-constitutional terms are going to get less specific. The only other option is the "constitutional death" of the larger family – it will cease to exist. Does this mean an illegitimate kind of compromise is necessary? Not necessarily. First of all, remember that the vertical family has priority over the horizontal family – better to have faithfulness passed onto a few families over time than the clan to grow large numerically but be characteristically unfaithful. Also, the point is not preserving a founding family's vision in and of itself. The focal point ought to be the expansion of the kingdom of God. What if the founding family's understanding of the kingdom of God was severely warped? I would hope the descendants would recognize this and mature its understanding and articulation of its mission.

Still, pragmatically, large families must deal with their diversity. The theory that I propose is one of descending specificity in higher levels of family constitutions. If a higher level of the family cannot accept all the specifics of the lower levels (clan to extended family, extended family to nuclear family), they can create a compact and constitution that is less specific but mutually agreeable. I'm using the term, *compact*, to acknowledge an agreement may fall short of a full covenant depending on the nature of the disagreements.

I propose that the "lowest common denominator" for such a compact is a compact to guard the larger family's life, liberty, and property. This idea has support from two sources. One is from James Hughes' recommendation that family governance systems model the republican systems that originally had as their goal the preservation of its citizens' life, liberty and property. A compact around this goal theoretically could even be made with unbelievers.

The second source is from 1 Timothy 5:8. This Scripture seems to suggest that Christian families are obligated to care for their relatives' material needs regardless of whether they are Christians or not. This would seem to warrant a confessional commitment (compact) to guard the larger family's material needs in whatever way is appropriate.

Consider how this theory could be applied to the following complex scenario: A group of five extended families are ready to become a clan. Four of those extended families are united around the specifics of the founding generation's covenant and constitution while one is not. Should that one extended family "spoil" the other four's ability to retain the original covenant? In this case, the four families could consider creating a *covenantal* clan with their four families based on continuity with the original multigenerational family vision. They may then consider an alliance or compact with the fifth family with more basic terms. Yes, this adds complexity, but without it, clans cannot accommodate the complex diversity that necessarily and naturally exists with such growth.

Conflict Resolution

We have already established that effective family governance is the often-overlooked key to multigenerational success. This implies that your family is able to communicate and get along with each other. Experience tells us this is rare and a very difficult goal to achieve. It is not an understatement to say that the inability of your family to effectively manage relational conflict is one of the greatest liabilities to the prospect of multigenerational success (recall the concept of the family balance sheet).

The default strategy of extended families is to avoid conflict at all costs even if it means sacrificing truth and genuine restoration. It is hoped that conflict will not occur. This is naïve and dangerous to your family. The first step in addressing the threat of conflict in your family is to expect it and plan for it. Successful multigenerational families have written-down conflict resolution plans and so should yours. Some of these families incorporate this component into their family constitution. Others have a separate document to deal with the subject.

To begin thinking about your family plan for conflict resolution, there is no reason why the pattern of Matthew 18 should not apply to your family. The vast majority of grievances should be dealt with between the parties directly affected. If that does not resolve the conflict, the next step is to bring in two or three others for help with mediation. Only if that process does not work should the matter be brought formally before a family council. While escalation to that level should be a rare event, it is important that the process is formally acknowledged (written down) so that family members know what remedies are available to them.

Many of the multigenerational family experts say that the elders of the family should especially be used for family conflict resolution. They have the experienced wisdom and, more often, enough detached objectivity to effectively play this mediating role.

It is important that family members are taught and encouraged that if they have a problem with another family member, it is their personal responsibility to initiate reconciliation. In many cases the other party is oblivious to the conflict.

For severe conflicts involving several family members, utilizing outside mediation help is advisable. Rather than wait for such a conflict to occur, seek out this mediator now. He will be an advisor on your family team and can help cultivate healthy relationships; prevention is always better than reaction.

We needed to highlight the basic point that your family needs to adopt a conflict resolution plan. However, this is not a manual on the specifics of how to do this. There are several great resources that will help your family accomplish this goal. Like many other areas, this will be another assignment in building your multigenerational family.

Chapter 6

A LOOK AHEAD

It is time to introduce those subjects that will have to wait until a later volume for their full discussion. I must confess, it pains me to know this volume does not address all that parents must know to build the foundation for their multigenerational family. I trust in God's providence that He has good reasons for this that I cannot foresee.

Family Discipleship Aimed at Generational Succession

The subject of the discipleship of family members is too important to leave to an introduction in this volume. While I have much research still unfinished, I could not let this book be released without laying down some foundations. As such, I've included an article titled, *Family Discipleship for Multigenerational Families* in the appendix. For those who need it, I pray that article will be sufficient to help place your family's education on a more biblical platform rather than the model offered by our pagan world. In the meantime, let us look at some subjects on multigenerational family discipleship anticipated in our upcoming volume.

Family discipleship is "where the action is at" in terms of the week-to-week practice of living multigenerational faithfulness. Recall from our discussion on the elements of a biblical covenant that covenantal continuity, or generational succession, was achieved by faithful discipleship of the living generation. No discipleship, no future faithful generations.

At present, the sections of this anticipated chapter will be broken up as follows—family rhythms, a Christian philosophy of education, and what I call generational training.

Family rhythms are the life context in which a family practices its more "formal" aspects of the discipleship of their children. Rhythms have to do with how a family structures its time. The structuring of time for Christian families begins with the week based on the Sabbath principle. From there, families structure their time in one direction to the smaller units of days and in the opposite direction to months, seasons, and annual and lifetime rhythms.

Among other considerations, a uniquely *Christian philosophy of education* understands education as discipleship. Whether or not parents utilize a private Christian school, from the perspective of multigenerational family planning, parents need to understand that they *alone* are responsible to create a discipleship and academic curriculum for their children (the Deuteronomy 6 principle). There are many resources on family discipleship. A book on multigenerational families will not pretend to duplicate this general and broad subject. Because the essence of multigenerational planning is all about governance, our discussion will focus on helping parents draft a comprehensive discipleship plan for their family.

I mentioned family rhythms above as a kind of necessary life context for Christian family education. Recently, it has come to my attention that there is another kind of context that our education needs to be enveloped in, and without which, our education will be in vain. The first principle is that right worship precedes right belief.[1] Consider the Church of the first four centuries. She was singing the praises of the Triune God long before she came to understand and articulate her belief in the Trinity during the fourth century. The other principle is that right relationships among family members must be in place if education is going to be effectively godly and fruitful. These themes will be elaborated on in our future volume.

The topic of family discipleship typically assumes children as the students in question. Multigenerational families, however, practice life-long learning for all of their members. They don't just ask how to raise godly children; they ask how they will raise up competent elders. With what can be called *generational training*, we will look at those subjects and activities that multigenerational families need to have more than an average competency in. Every family member of a maturing generational family will need to become a competent fiduciary and trustee of valuable human and economic wealth.

Building and Preserving Generational Wealth

A false piety among some Christians may yield an assumption that they can build and preserve a multigenerational family without giving attention to the financial wealth of their family. Their worry about the corrupting potential of wealth is admirable, but their conclusion is wrong. When we discuss this subject, we will begin by making the necessary distinction between a godly pursuit of wealth with the (unfortunately more common) ungodly pursuit of wealth. We will show why pursuing economic wealth is absolutely necessary (and biblical) for families to preserve their family heritage over the generations.

We will discuss the idea of starting a traditional family business. However, a distinction needs to be recognized between active businesses operated by households with the "family business" of the multigenerational family. The multigenerational "family business" is the growth, preservation, and distribution of its economic assets. From an accounting perspective, those assets are passive. For example, a family trust may own an active business, but there's a difference from managing that asset in terms of ownership, as opposed to the active operations conducted by the business's managers. It is no different than the way a trust or individual owns stocks—it's "passive" management as an investment.

I also want to discuss the subject of disinheritance under this theme. Assuming it is true that there is a distinction between the covenantal multigenerational family and the biological multigenerational family, what makes a biological family member cease to be part of the covenantal multigenerational family? By definition of biblical covenants, they must be covenantally removed. Again, using biblical-covenantal terms, this would constitute covenantal disinheritance. While this will most likely take place by a governmental decision of the family council (or by a father), covenantal concepts also ask for a corresponding ritual or sign to accompany this disinheritance. In the Church, that sign is the barring of the former church member from taking communion—excommunication. Biblically, a pattern you see in family heads "excommunicating" sons is literally disinheritance—not passing the economic assets of the father to the son. This seems to correspond to the need for a ritual sign when a change in the covenant takes place. *If this is all true, it may be the strongest argument for the connection between a family's spiritual multigenerational mission and the economic assets of a family.*

I will also be discussing what I call the paradox of family preservation. On the one hand: at least from the economic perspective, multigenerational families need to focus on preservation rather than growth. Hence, a very long-term and *conservative* investment strategy needs to be employed. Individual entrepreneurs may have the prerogative to risk big and lose, but multigenerational families do not have this luxury. Preservation is paramount, especially through hazardous times.

On the other hand: there is a uniform message I have learned from such authors as Alan Hirsch, in *The Forgotten Ways*, and Nicholas Talib, in *The Black Swan* (it is also beautifully portrayed in the movie, *Defiance*). The takeaway from these sources is that those who survived hazardous times were not living in the previously safe center of the mainstream. They lived on "the edge of chaos." They were neither in full chaos where destruction is likely, nor the "safe, conservative," center mainstream that is only safe as long as the previous environment holds. New environments kill those who cannot adapt (think of goldfish!). Multigenerational families need to live out this paradox of conservatism and pioneering risk at the same time.

In addition to the above, a review of traditional portfolio theory will be discussed followed by what makes investing for a multigenerational family different from traditional methods (short-term vs. long-term time horizons). The Austrian school of economics and the "Alpha Strategy" will be explained. The role of dynasty trusts will be explained and encouraged (aka, generation-skipping trusts, or perpetual trusts). The role of professional advisors will be addressed as well.

The Horizontal Family: Extended Family, Clan, and Tribe

The term, "horizontal family," refers to the living generation of a family (from extended family to tribe) in contrast to the "vertical family," which is the multigenerational family that exists abstractly throughout time. While multigenerational disciplines are focused on the vertical family, the experts have observed that no successful multigenerational families have neglected maturing the strength of their horizontal family from generation to generation. The fact is, the growth and strength of the horizontal family is one of the key contributors to success of the vertical, multigenerational family.

This future chapter will discuss the nature of these larger elements of the horizontal family. We will uncover the relationships between the different levels of the horizontal family – nuclear, extended, clan and tribe. Most attention will be given to the clan as that is the level at which today's new multigenerational families need to learn to develop.

We will explore the relationship of the family with the other covenantal institutions of the church and the state. We will need to return to the topic of proper jurisdictions. There is much confusion on what rights and privileges belong to each of these covenantal institutions. We will address criticisms of the idea that families should even seek to become clans and tribes.

Roles

As mentioned in previous discussions, when the Bible talks about families, it does not assume the individualistic, nuclear families of our modern, Western culture. While it sees distinctions between what we call nuclear families and broader relationships (using different terminology), the tendency is to see the locus of what family means in much broader terms. For example, household servants would often be considered family members.

To consider another example to reveal this ancient-modern contrast, consider the elevated roles of extended family members in a covenantal family. Grandfathers are still covenantally obligated to see both their adult children and grandchildren are discipled. Yes, it looks different than fathers, but it is still there. And consider the implications a theology of the kinsmen-redeemer has on aunts and uncles. Grandparents, aunts and uncles have much more specific and vitally necessary roles in multigenerational families. It is necessary for multi-generational families to learn what are the covenantal obligations (and rights) of fathers, mothers, sons, daughters, siblings, cousins, aunts and uncles, grandparents, in-laws, and, yes, even employees of the family. They will also need to define roles for family members appointed to governing offices.

Under this subject heading we will also categorize the different areas of expertise a family will want to gain access to. This is not an exhaustive list, but such roles will include experts in the following areas: legal, financial, educational, medical, risk management, technology, politics, and the manual trades. At first, access to most of those areas of specialty will need to be obtained through outside advisors. Over time (generationally) multigenerational families should identify and groom individual family members to become experts in those different specialty disciplines.

Generational Growth and Maturity

Christians typically recognize that individuals can (at least should) mature over their lifetimes. What is not sufficiently recognized is that covenantal communities (families, churches, and nations) can (and should) mature over generations (beyond the scope of an individual lifetime). What is also not sufficiently recognized is that individual maturity is radically dependent on, and conditioned by, the maturity of one's community. Multigenerational families need to have a vision of not only maturing their own family over time but their communities as well – ecclesiastical and civic. The maturity of their future family has a direct proportional relationship to the maturity of the ecclesiastical and civil communities in which they live. This subject will be developed in our future release.

The Generational Family in Kingdom Context

This subject may very well be incorporated into the theme of the Horizontal Family and its relationship to the Church. The message of the book as a whole may suggest to readers that multigenerational-family-building is more comprehensive than is warranted. It is our historical situation that has called for a renewed emphasis on the biblical family. The task of multigenerational faithfulness is indeed a glorious and comprehensive thing, however, it can easily be pursued in an ungodly manner and blind families from larger realities. Among other considerations, families need to see the eternal nature of the Church as the Bride of Christ. Eschatologically, our earthly families are temporal and will be incorporated into the one family of God. Without this perspective, families are in danger of making an idol of the family.

Appendix

FAMILY DISCIPLESHIP FOR MULTIGENERATIONAL FAMILIES

Christian parenting as it relates to building a multigenerational dynasty for Kingdom impact will be focused on the idea of a *comprehensive discipleship curriculum*. To successfully transmit your family's mission and culture necessarily implies that Christian parents will adequately train their children in that mission and culture.

Defining Terms

We need to start out by defining some terms. There are three alternate terms we could use to identify the concept we are talking about here. We could variably talk either about an,
- *education* curriculum, a
- *training* curriculum, or
- a *discipleship* curriculum.

Each of those terms applies to what we will be talking about. And while much of what those terms convey overlap with each other, they also have their separate, distinct emphases. The idea of education emphasizes there is a body of knowledge to master. It points to content. It might also entail the idea of a curriculum as well. Finally, relative to the other terms, education is more closely associated with what we call academic subjects. All of these connotations are elements Christian parents will want to incorporate in their family training program.

The common association of *education*, however, by itself, can have certain limitations. Specifically, it can convey the idea of merely head knowledge. It doesn't have to do this, but it often does. Therefore, the concept of *training* helps overcome that often limiting connotation found in the term, *education*. With training, we expect a person to not only know something, but know *how* to do something. Consider a pilot. It makes much more sense to us to talk about a pilot's *training*, rather than a pilot's *education*. His education isn't for the purpose of merely knowing *about* planes, but rather *how* to fly planes. Training is a much closer concept for what Christian parents should be thinking of in terms of raising their children for multigenerational kingdom impact. It is training *to do* certain things, not merely know certain things. With this said, I don't want to give the impression that training is necessarily a "better" idea than education. The terms just have different emphases. For example, the concept of training does not have the comprehensive connotation that the word education conveys, and we want to retain that concept as well.

Given the limitations found in the concepts of education and training, it is perhaps more advantageous to use the term discipleship for this context. For starters, discipleship carries the idea of mentoring oneself to a person rather than to merely a system, content, set of skills or ideology. For Christian parents this is a superior focal point. Our multigenerational family building is not for ourselves or for our family, but for a Kingdom. A Kingdom has a King and that King is Jesus. We are stewards of God's Kingdom. We are but tutors, apprenticing our children to the One Master, Jesus Christ. The other reason why discipleship may be the better of the terms is that it is more comprehensive. It includes the content-focused idea of education and the skill development-orientation of training, but those terms can lack other aspects of training that discipleship helps convey. Discipleship carries with it aspects of faith training, character training, training of our affections and more. Again, we are not saying those other terms cannot carry those ideas, but some words have stronger connotations than others and may be more useful in certain contexts.

Now what about those words surrounding discipleship, in our key phrase, *"comprehensive discipleship curriculum"*? The terms *comprehensive* and *curriculum* may be somewhat overlapping. Curriculum conveys the idea of a plan. You, as Christian parents, are responsible for the work of formulating a plan for the discipleship of your children. That plan will include determining what subjects they are to be trained in, and when. The term, *comprehensive*, implies that you will intend to not leave out any critical component to that plan. If you are only beginning to make such a plan you may feel overwhelmed by this prospect. Let me alleviate some of that concern. This is going to take some time, and it is okay that it is going to take time. You are a pioneer. You will find you are not going to be able to implement some things in your or your children's own generation. Here is one of the beauties of multigenerational thinking. You don't have to complete everything in your own generation. As a matter of fact, you can't! But you can begin to build the foundation. Begin the foundation and your children and your children's children will build upon it.

Categorizing Education and Family Rhythms

In a moment, we will look at a recommended model of a comprehensive discipleship curriculum. Before we do, two preliminary matters need to be discussed – first, a Christian philosophy of education (especially as it relates to categorizing the entire field of learning) and second, the nature of what I call *family rhythms*.

A Christian Philosophy of Education. Part of a Christian discipleship curriculum will include what most people commonly think of as "the school subjects" – math, English, history, science, art, etc. Perhaps the most common label to cover this diversity of learning is the term, "the liberal arts." While such terminology may be acceptable as long as it is understood within a biblical worldview, without such a biblical worldview, such terms have anti-biblical philosophical assumptions built into them that most of us are unaware of (indeed, most Christians do not possess an adequate biblical worldview).

From Greco-Roman antiquity, the term *liberal* in, "the liberal arts," meant *free*. A *liberal* education, then, was meant the education that is fitting for a free person (as opposed to a slave). This tells us what the ancient Greeks thought of as the main *purpose* of education – to equip a man to both maintain his freedom and contribute to the freedom of his society. Now this is actually a significantly better purpose than the current purpose of American education – Christians included! The American purpose of education is to equip a person to be a productive worker in society. If you disagree, I do not have the space here to make that argument (I do that elsewhere). But be honest, why are most Christian families today deathly afraid if their kids do not go to college? Because if they don't, they won't be able make enough money to support a desired lifestyle. Christian parents are not typically afraid that their kids' education will fail to produce the fear of God in them. Reverse-engineer this and the truth is, Christian parents *really* believe education is about making the right amount of money! (Let's not deceive ourselves. Don't check what your mind consciously tells you what you believe; check your behavior or your emotional attitude.)

While those ancient Greeks at least knew better than this (freedom is at least a higher value than security), they still fall short of the biblical purpose of what we call education. This will sound like a superficial cliché at first, but trust me, the reality is much more profound than most people realize. In the biblical assumption, the ultimate purpose of education is the knowledge of God (things like *freedom* and *security* ought to be secondary and tertiary by-products).

According to a biblical worldview, when we study what we most commonly call "the school subjects," we are actually studying God's creation. God designed everything in each piece of His creation to reveal specific things. "Education," or "learning," is about discovering those things. What we think of as education, or learning, today is nothing other than an expression of the command God gave Adam to name the animals. Learning is about distinguishing and identifying. This is exactly what Adam was to do and it continues to be our educational and cultural mandate.

We have a terminology problem today in the Christian world. We don't have a good, biblically faithful term to label the study of "the school subjects." Indeed, in our family homeschooling endeavors we used to say, "It's time to do school." The primary connotation of "school" today is an invention of pagan intellectuals who included in their aims the destruction of Christianity! Our family now calls it "academics," but that is only because we don't have a better alternative. In substance, what we are doing is studying creation, but we don't have a culturally meaningful term, like "creationics" or "the creation arts." Perhaps, with Christians practicing multigenerational dominion faithfulness, a new, biblically faithful term will be coined in the next generation that will garner cultural traction. In the meantime, I will use the label, "academics," to refer to what we normally think of as the liberal arts, or "the school subjects" – math, English, history, science, etc. Just know that I'm defining it to mean a study of God's creation.

The *above* explanation is actually a brief summary. Let me recommend the following two books, which will explain and make this argument for Christian parents. The first is <u>The Myth of Religious Neutrality</u> by Roy Clouser. The fact that most Christians believe they can have their children educated by the public school in a "neutral" way is evidence that they have been deceived by this Luciferean doctrine of religious neutrality. Hey, "1+1=2 no matter where or how you learn it, right?" Try asking your public school math teacher, "What *is* a number?" and watch him or her squirm. The number '1' is a creation of God. That is the most important thing to know about numbers, about "math." When you go through twelve years of this kind of godless math (to use just this one example), it desensitizes the mind and robs God of His glory. The second book is <u>Reclaiming the Future of Christian Education</u> by Albert Greene. I consider this "mandatory reading" for every Christian parent.

Categorization. Categorizing things is a necessary activity to help us better understand different aspects of an otherwise unified whole. Remember, this is part of what Adam was called to do by distinguishing between the different kinds of animals. It is important to consider that *discipleship training* is a unity with diverse elements. When we transition from what I will call *faith training* to *academics*, for example, we are not making a jump across a giant chasm. They fundamentally belong to a similar nature, or at least are more similar than they are different. We'll see this in more specificity when we describe these two elements below.

Family Rhythms. This article is focused on what we're calling a discipleship curriculum. However, it needs to be mentioned here that family rhythms provide the foundational life structure or context around which family discipleship training takes place. We believe family rhythms start with the week and from there work to the smaller components of days and towards the opposite direction of months, seasons, years, and lifetimes. Family rhythms include such things as daily family worship, weekly family Sabbath observance, and annual celebrations. These rhythmic patterns are a necessary context in which to conduct your family discipleship.

Curriculum Overview

In *what* follows, I am going to offer a model, or outline, of a comprehensive discipleship curriculum for a multigenerational family. I am discussing the *structure* of a discipleship curriculum, not the specific *contents*. There are dozens of ways one could categorize such a curriculum. There are essential, core principles that can be expressed and categorized in different ways, and there are other aspects that will be unique to each individual family. The below outline is a top-level view.

Here is how I'm currently categorizing and labeling our family's discipleship curriculum from the bird's-eye view: Foundational Training, which is broadly sub-categorized into (i) Faith Training and (ii) Academic Training. The other main category I have come to label as Generational Training with the sub-categories of (i) Family Mission Training; (ii) Business and Financial Training; (iii) Manual Skills Training; and (iv) Experiential Opportunities and Events.

I have admittedly had a very difficult time labeling and summarizing the learning categories beyond Foundational Training that I think are important for multigenerational families to distinguish and identify. Indeed some of them can properly be considered sub-sets of academic training. What I came to realize is that these subjects are important to be elevated to a more conscious level from the perspective of multigenerational family thinking specifically (which is why I eventually have chosen the label of "Generational Training").

For example, business and financial training is a category that I have identified as distinct for our multigenerational family. Why? I have learned from studies on successful multigenerational families that all family members need to have a higher sophistication of business and financial matters than the average person. Finance is a sub-set of economics, and economics is properly within the field of academic study. However, while there is a general learning of economics that is appropriate for every generally educated person, a multigenerational family member needs a higher level of sophistication in this area, as they will be responsible for decisions that affect large sums of money.

In outline form then, our family discipleship structure looks like this:

   I. Foundational Training
      a. Faith Training
      b. Academic Training
  II. Generational Training
      a. Family Mission Training
      b. Business and Financial Training
      c. Manual Skills Training
      d. Experiential Opportunities and Events

Let me re-emphasize one more time. This is *our current* family structure and it gets tweaked from time to time. I'm not proposing that this should be every Christian family's outline. This is just a training tool to help families create their own structures. Yes, there are some core principles here, but those can be expressed and organized in a variety of ways.

Faith Training

By "faith training" I mean, of course, training in the Christian faith. I could use other terms like, "Bible training" or "spiritual training," but those don't convey what we mean here. Faith training for children will seek to familiarize them with the entire story of the Bible. In Christian homes, by the time children are young adults they should be *very* familiar with the basic content of the entirety of the Scriptures. This implies years of reading large portions of the Scriptures, both together as a family and directed personal reading.

There will also be a chatechistic component to faith training. There are core doctrines and highlights of God's story that children need to be well grounded in. Catechistic training can take many forms. The important thing is that whatever form is chosen, it is done.

Another reason why I prefer the label *faith training* is that it points to the truth that we are not training for mere knowledge. This is training for wisdom, character, and well — faith! Particularly, the wisdom, character, and faith of Jesus Christ.

Multigenerational parent trainers will also recognize how the pattern of Deuteronomy chapter 6 plays into this. The commandants of the LORD are to be talked about with your children as you "sit in your house, and when you walk by the way, and when you lie down, and when you rise." This is why only parents can be the primary educators of their children. Who else is going to be with your children when they "sit, walk, lie down, and rise"?

The book of Proverbs is another focal point as it is specifically designed for training children in the wisdom of God.

You may be thinking this is just plain 'ol Christian discipleship of children, and what does it have to do with multigenerational family building? On the one hand, you're right. This is basic Christian discipleship. Here's what I want you to see, however. Most families' focal point is that we train our children for their own personal spiritual lives. So they can "be good Christians." That's fine as far as it goes. But Christian parents need to transcend that over-personalized focus and see the bigger picture. You must catch a vision for building competent soldiers for Jesus Christ who will be increasingly effective in Kingdom work from generation to generation. Speaking personally, once I gained this vision, my motivation to "diligently teach my children the commandants of the LORD" (Deut. 6:7) increased exponentially.

Academic Training

I have already described the essence of what we're calling academic training above. Delving deeper into this subject is appropriate for another context, however, there is an additional higher-level perspective that needs to be mentioned here. Families today, Christian or otherwise, assume that academics is the only kind of work children are to engage in until, at least, their teen years. The case is not to be argued in this brief overview, however, many Christian families today are beginning to see that we've lost the value of good 'ol fashioned "work-work" for children. And I mean more than mere chores. Chores are maintenance. I'm talking productivity. Children need to be engaged in productive work as part of their daily and weekly rhythms. Academics is just one kind of work rhythm. In our family, academics is one work rhythm and productive work is another rhythm (see *family rhythms* above).

Generational Training

Family Mission Training: In addition to the foundation core discussed above, a family will train in their family mission. This assumes of course you have a family mission. Our family trains in our family mission every Sabbath.

Business and Financial Training: Why do I list Business and Financial Training as a subject that should be included in every multigenerational family's discipleship curriculum? Simply, because your family is already an economic enterprise, whether you recognize it or not. Multigenerational families are asset builders and preservers. This necessarily implies the need to obtain the corresponding skills.

Manual Skills: Basic manual skills should be included as part of a family's training curriculum for their children. All children should be trained to maintain a household and be trained in what it means to work hard and work with excellence. Boys are growing up to be men. They should be taught basic hand-to-hand and firearms self-defense skills. They should have a basic competency in common household repairs. Girls should learn basic cooking skills. These are just some examples. You will need to determine for your family what to put on this list.

Experiential Opportunities and Events: Finally, children should be given certain opportunities and experience certain events. I don't have any sort of definitive list in mind, but some examples would include participation in real debates, traveling on their own at age-appropriate times, and starting their own micro-business. I am also becoming increasingly convinced that multigenerational families need to resurrect the coming of age ceremonies that our ancestors practiced. We do not need to follow the culture that leads youth into a vague adulthood of self-discovery where hopefully, someday they learn to become a man or woman. Our ancestors knew what they were doing when they trained their children to become men and women and determined a season that culminated in a ceremony that drew the line in the sand that told the world, today John is a man; today, Cindy is a woman.

In Closing

This may all seem daunting and overwhelming. I have not mentioned yet the role of contracting out some of this discipleship workload. As Christian parents we are responsible for the training of our children, but that does not mean we will be the exclusive direct trainers in every little area. While the core issues of wisdom, character, and faith training cannot be contracted out, with God's wisdom we will discern what parts we can contract out to others.

BIBLIOGRAPHY

Christian Multigenerational Family

Pryor, Jeremy, *ReFamily: The Biblical Blueprint*. Accessed January 7, 2014. http://www.pathsofreturn.com/refamily-the-bibles-blueprint/.

Schwartz, Andrea. The Biblical Trustee Family: Understanding God's Purpose for Your Household. Vallecito, California: Chalcedon/Ross House Books, 2010.

Wikner, Benjamin K. To You and Your Children: Examining the Biblical Doctrine of Covenant Succession. Moscow, Idaho: Canon Press, 2005.

Willis, Norman. The Ancient Path: A Return to the Kingdom Mandate of Generational Transfer. 2^d ed. Kirkland, WA: Christ Church Publishing, 1998.

General Multigenerational Family

Bonner, Bill and Will Bonner. Family Fortunes: How to Build Family Wealth and Hold on to It for 100 Years. Hoboken, NJ: John Wiley & Sons, 2012.

Brower, Lee. The Brower Quadrant: Live Life Deliberately. USA: Lee Brower, 2009.

Gersick, Kelin E., et. al. Generation to Generation: Life Cycles of the Family Business. Boston, MA: Harvard Business School Press, 1997.

Hausner, Lee, and Douglas K. Freeman. The Legacy Family: The Definitive Guide to Creating a Successful Multigenerational Family. New York, NY: Palgrave MacMillan, 2009.

Hughes, James E. Jr. Family Wealth: Keeping It in the Family: How Family Members and Their Advisors Preserve Human, Intellectual, and Financial Assets for Generations. 2nd ed. Princeton, NJ: Bloomberg Press, 2004.

. Family:The Compact Among Generations: Answers and Insights from a Lifetime of Helping Families Flourish. New York, NY: Bloomberg Press, 2007.

Lansberg, Ivan. Succeeding Generations: Realizing the Dream of Families in Business. Boston, MA: Harvard Business School Press, 1999.

Ottinger, Randall J. Beyond Success: Building a Personal, Financial, and Philanthropic Legacy. New York, NY: McGraw-Hill, 2008.

Covenant Family Discipleship

Alexander, James W. Thoughts on Family Worship. Ed. Don Kistler. Originally published by Presbyterian Board of Publication: 1847. Morgan, PA: Soli Deo Gloria Publications, 1998.

Garr, John D. PhD. Family Sanctuary: Restoring the Biblically Hebraic Home. Atlanta, GA: Restoration Foundation, 2003.

Hess, Richard S. and Daniel Carroll R. eds. Family in the Bible: Exploring Customs, Culture, and Context. Grand Rapids, MI: Baker Academic, 2003.

Hill, Craig. Bar Barakah: A Parent's Guide to a Christian Bar Mitzvah. Littleton, CO: Family Foundations International, 1998.

Kostenberger, Andreas J. with David W. Jones. God, Marriage and Family: Rebuilding the Biblical Foundation. 2d ed. Wheaton, IL: Crossway, 2004, 2010.

Lancaster, Philip. Family Man, Family Leader: Biblical Fatherhood as the Key to a Thriving Family. San Antonio, TX: The Vision Forum, Inc. 2003, 2007.

Lewis, Robert. Raising a Modern-Day Knight: A Father's Role in Guiding His Son to Authentic Manhood. Revised. Carol Stream, IL: Tyndale House Publishers, 1997, 2007.

Matthew, Cotton. A Family Well-Ordered. Ed. Don Kistler. First published in Boston, MA in 1699. Morgan, PA: Soli Deo Gloria Publications, 2001.

Maxwell, Steven. Preparing Sons to Provide for a Single-Income Family. Leavenworth, Kansas: Communication Concepts, 2001.

Sutton, Ray R. That You May Prosper: Dominion by Covenant. Tyler, TX: Institute for Christian Economics, 1987.

Wilson, Douglas. Standing on the Promises: A Handbook of Biblical Childrearing. Moscow, ID: Canon Press, 1997.

Wilson, Douglas. Reforming Marriage. Moscow, ID: Canon Press, 1995.

Christian Education

Greene, Albert E. Reclaiming the Future of Christian Education: A Transforming Vision. Colorado Springs, Colorado: Association of Christian Schools International, 1998.

Mulligan, David. Far Above Rubies: Wisdom in the Christian Community. Marshfield, Vermont: Messenger Publishing, 1994.

Rushdoony, Rousas John. The Philosophy of the Christian Curriculum. Vallecito, California: Ross House Books, 1981.

Sproul Jr., R. C.. When You Rise Up: A Covenantal Approach to Homeschooling. Phillisburg, New Jersey: P&R Publishing, 2004.

Family Economics

Pugsley, John A. 2d ed. The Alpha Strategy: The Ultimate Plan of Financial Self-Defense. Los Angles, CA: Stratford Press, 1980, 1981.

Other

Crawford, John G. Baptism is Not Enough: How Understanding God's Covenant Explains Everything. Powder Springs, GA: American Vision Press, 2013.

Bibliography

Gentry, Peter J. and Stephen J. Wellum. <u>Kingdom through Covenant: A Biblical-Theological Understanding of the Covenants.</u> Wheaton, IL: Crossway, 2012.

Strauss, D F M. <u>Philosophy: Discipline of the Disciplines</u>. Grand Rapids, MI: Paideia Press, 2009.

Woods, Dennis. <u>Disciple the Nations: The Government Upon His Shoulder</u>. Franklin, TN: Legacy Communications, 1996.

Zimmerman, Carle C. <u>Family and Civilization</u>. Originally published New York: Harper, 1947. 2nd printing Wilmington, DE: ISI Books, 2008.

END NOTES

Chapter 1

[1] Norman Willis, The Ancient Path: A Return to the Kingdom Mandate of Generational Transfer. 2^d ed. (Kirkland, WA: Christ Church Publishing, 1998), 20.

[2] Jeremy Pryor, *ReFamily: The Biblical Blueprint*. http://www.pathsofreturn.com/refamily-the-bibles-blueprint/, 2014.

[3] Ibid.

[4] Carle C. Zimmerman, Family and Civilization 2nd ed. (New York: Harper, 1947), 22-23.

[5] Zimmerman., 25.

[6] Zimmerman., 27.

[7] Zimmerman., 30-31.

[8] R. J. Rushdoony, The Institutes of Biblical Law: Law and Society. vol. 2. (Vallecito: Ross House Books, 1982), 43.

[9] Rushdoony., 387.

[10] Ray Sutton, That You May Prosper: Dominion By Covenant (Tyler, TX: Institute for Christian Economics, 1987), 18.

[11] Sutton, 16-17. Sutton also recognizes Meredith G. Kline's exposition of ancient Near East suzerainty covenants following this pattern: Preamble, Historical

Prologue, Stipulations, Blessing and Cursing, Successional Arrangements, and Depository Arrangements (*The Structure of Biblical Authority*).

[12] Milton C. Fisher quoting Gary North in Foreword to Sutton, xi.

[13] This section adapted from Sutton, 105-117.

[14] Sutton, 108.

[15] Daniel C. Lane, "The Meaning and Use of the Old Testament Term for 'Covenant' (*berit*) with Some Implications for Dispensationalism and Covenant Theology" (PhD diss,. Trinity International University, 2000). Adapted quote from Peter J. Gentry and Stephen J. Wellum, <u>Kingdom through Covenant: A Biblical-Theological Understanding of the Covenants</u> (Wheaton, IL: Crossway, 2012), 132.

[16] First inner quotation by John A. Davies, "A Royal Priesthood: Literary and Intertextual Perspectives on an Image of Israel in Exodus" *19:6*, JSOTSup 395 (London: T. & T. Clark, 2004), 175-176 . Whole quote from, Gentry and Wellum, <u>Kingdom through Covenant</u>,133.

[17] James B. Jordan, <u>The Law of the Covenant</u> (Tyler, TX: Institute for Christian Economics, 1984), 4.

[18] John G. Crawford, <u>Baptism is Not Enough: How Understanding God's Covenant Explains Everything</u>, (Powder Springs, GA: American Vision Press, 2013), 23.

[19] Sutton, 144.

[20] Gentry and Wellum. 155.

[21] Sutton, 116.

[22] Sutton, 2.

[23] Norm Willis,<u>The Ancient Path: A Return to the Kingdom Mandate of Generational Transfer</u> 2nd ed. (Kirkland, WA: Christ Church Publishing, 1999, 2006).

[24] James E. Hughes Jr. Family Wealth: Keeping It in the Family, 2d ed. (Princeton, NJ: Bloomberg Press, 2004), 3.

[25] Rushdoony, 43.

[26] Hughes, xv.

[27] Lee Hausner and Douglas Freeman, The Legacy Family: The Definitive Guide to Creating a Successful Multigenerational Family (New York: Palgrave MacMillian, 2009), 17.

Chapter 2

[1] Hauser and Freeman, 169-175.

Chapter 3

[1] Hughes, 6.

[2] http://mtjohnson.com/news/strategic-planning-the-basics/ (2014).

[3] http://en.wikipedia.org/wiki/Strategic_planning (2014).

[4] Pryor, Re-Family: The Biblical Blueprint, http://www.paths-ofreturn.com. (2014).

[5] Willis, 27.

[6] Ibid., 35.

[7] Ibid,. 35-36.

[8] Ibid,. 62.

[9] Ibid., 64.

[10] Ibid,., 182-183.

[11] See chapter on Governance for why I specify sons rather than both sons and daughters.

[12] Gentry and Wellum, Kingdom Through Covenant.

[13] Willis, 197.

End Notes

[14] Pryor, Re-Family: The Biblical Blueprint, http://www.pathsofreturn.com.

[15] Willis, 42.

[16] Willis, 176.

[17] Willis, 176, 181.

[18] Sample statements 1 and 2 are taken from Norm Willis' book, The Ancient Path: A Return to the Kingdom Mandate of Generational Transfer. Sample statements 3-5 were graciously provided by friends and family.

[19] http://en.wikipedia.org/wiki/Strategic_planning (2014).

Chapter 4

[1] Hughes, xv.

[2] Ibid., 8.

[3] Ibid., 58.

[4] Ibid,. 60.

[5] Lee Brower, The Brower Quadrant: Live Life Deliberately (self-published, 2009), 48.

[6] Hausner and Freeman, 7.

[7] Hughes, 19.

Chapter 5

[1] Hughes, 4.

[2] Sutton, 145.

[3] See below for why I think it is appropriate to reserve this discussion of jurisdictional boundaries to sons rather than both sons and daughters.

[4] See Sutton's quote on this from chapter 1.

⁵ Hughes, 24.

⁶ A republic as a form of governance emphasizes representation. A people elect from amongst themselves individuals to represent them in a governing body.

⁷ Note "republican" with a small 'r' refers to the system of governance; it does not refer to the Republican party of the modern American system.

⁸ Description of what a clan is, is discussed below.

⁹ http://davidbork.com/2012/11/consensus-decision-making-in-family-business/ (2014).

¹⁰ Ibid (2014).

¹¹ The double-portion principle means the firstborn receives double what each of his brothers receive from their father's estate. For example, in a family with three sons, the firstborn receives half of the estate and the other two sons each receive a quarter.

¹² Douglas Wilson, <u>Reforming Marriage</u> (Moscow: Canon Press), 37.

¹³ Capitalized terms are defined terms in our family constitution.

¹⁴ In our family the "founder" is obviously myself. It is more appropriate, however, to use the language of "founder" in this context rather than the personal pronoun.

¹⁵ At the time of this writing, I am thinking of lowering this age limit threshold.

¹⁶ Further explanation of what a clan is all about will be discussed in a future revision of this work. In the meantime, please connect with www.thecovenantfamilyinstitute.com for more information or questions.

¹⁷ This does not have to be the second grandson born from the Founder's chronologically firstborn grandson. It is literally

the second grandson, no matter from which grandson he comes from.

[18] D F M Strauss, Philosophy: Discipline of the Disciplines (Grand Rapids, MI: Paideia Press, 2009), 538-539.

[19] Dennis Woods, Disciple the Nations: The Government Upon His Shoulder (Franklin, TN: Legacy Communications, 1996), 142.

[20] Woods, 190-191.

Chapter 6

[1] See the works of James B. Jordan.

CPSIA information can be obtained
at www.ICGtesting.com
Printed in the USA
FSOW02n1748200317
32052FS